REJECTED PROPHETS

REJECTED PROPHETS

JESUS AND HIS WITNESSES
IN LUKE-ACTS

JOCELYN McWHIRTER

Fortress Press
Minneapolis

REJECTED PROPHETS

Jesus and His Witnesses in Luke-Acts

Scripture quotations are from the New Revised Standard Version Bible, copyright © 1989 by the Division of Christian Education of the National Council of the Churches of Christ in the USA. Used by permission. All rights reserved.

Cover image: Erich Lessing / Art Resource, NY

Cover design: Tory Herman

Library of Congress Cataloging-in-Publication Data

McWhirter, Jocelyn.

Rejected prophets : Jesus and his witnesses in Luke-Acts / Jocelyn McWhirter.

pages cm

Includes bibliographical references and index.

ISBN 978-1-4514-7002-4 (pbk. : alk. paper) — ISBN 978-1-4514-8026-9 (ebook)

1. Bible. Luke–Criticism, interpretation, etc. 2. Bible. Acts–Criticism, interpretation, etc. 3. Apostles–Biblical teaching. I. Title.

BS2589.M44 2013   226.4'06–dc23   2013034856

The paper used in this publication meets the minimum requirements of American National Standard for Information Sciences — Permanence of Paper for Printed Library Materials, ANSI Z329.48-1984.

Manufactured in the U.S.A.

This book was produced using PressBooks.com, and PDF rendering was done by PrinceXML.

For my parents,
who brought me to church
and sent me to school

CONTENTS

Abbreviations

1 Macc. 1 Maccabees
1Q28b *Rule of the Blessings*
2 Bar. *2 Baruch*
4QFlor *Florilegium*
4QpIsa^a *Isaiah Pesher^a*
ABRL Anchor Bible Reference Library
AnBib Analecta biblica
Ant. *Jewish Antiquities* (Josephus)
ANTC Abington New Testament Commentaries
BETL Bibliotheca ephemeridum theologicarum lovaniensium
Bib *Biblica*
FB Forschung zur Bibel
JBL *Journal of Biblical Literature*
JRS *Journal of Roman Studies*
J.W. *Jewish War* (Josephus)
LXX Septuagint
NA^{28} *Novum Testamentum Graece*, Nestle-Aland, 28th ed.
NICNT New International Commentary on the New Testament
NIV New International Version
NRSV New Revised Standard Version
NTL New Testament Library
NTS *New Testament Studies*
OTP *Old Testament Pseudepigrapha*. Edited by J. H. Charlesworth. 2 vols. New
  York, 1983
Pss. Sol. *Psalms of Solomon*
RHPR *Revue d'historie et de philosophie religieuses*
SBLDS Society of Biblical Literature Dissertation Series
SBLMS Society of Biblical Literature Monograph Series
SBLSP Society of Biblical Literature Seminar Papers
SNTSMS Society for New Testament Studies Monograph Series
SP Sacra pagina

StudNeot Studia neotestamentica

SubBi *Subsidio Biblica*

TBT *The Bible Today*

TDNT *Theological Dictionary of the New Testament.* Edited by G. Kittel and G. Friedrich. Translated by G. W. Bromiley. 10   vols. Grand Rapids, 1964-1976

T. Jud. *Testament of Judah*

T. Lev. *Testament of Levi*

TPINTC TPI New Testament Commentaries

WBC Word Biblical Commentary

WMANT Wissenschaftliche Monographien zum Alten und Neuen Testament

Introduction

This book got its start in a classroom at Saint Joseph's University. I was teaching Luke's Gospel for the first time. Since my graduate career had focused mainly on Paul, Mark, and John, this meant that I was seriously analyzing Luke's Gospel for the first time as well. I wanted to make sense of it, not only for my students but also for myself. What motivated the author? Who was his audience, and what was he trying to tell them?

Because writers emphasize what they want most to convey, I started with Luke's major themes—themes that continue into the Gospel's sequel, the book of Acts. These were easy enough to discern. Our textbook even provided a partial list.

- The work of the Holy Spirit
- Prayer
- Prominent female characters
- Concern for sinners, the disabled, and the poor
- Christianity as a legal religion
- God's plan of salvation—a plan that includes Gentiles as well as Jews
- Jesus as the Savior.[1]

In the interest of thoroughness, I thought I should complete the list for my students. I added a few more, mostly drawn from other textbooks.

- The frequent intervention of angels
- The fulfillment of the Scriptures[2]
- The centrality of Jerusalem[3]
- The salvation of Samaritans
- Jesus as the Messiah[4]

---

1. Stephen L. Harris, *The New Testament: A Student's Introduction*, 3rd ed. (Mountain View, CA: Mayfield, 1999), 164–66. For an earlier statement of the same ideas, see Henry J. Cadbury, *The Making of Luke-Acts*, 3rd ed. (Peabody, MA: Hendrickson, 1999), 254–69, 308–13. Cadbury's book was first published in 1927.

2. Mitchell G. Reddish, *An Introduction to the Gospels* (Nashville: Abingdon, 1997), 151.

3. Harris, *New Testament*, 159. Harris adds "Importance of Jerusalem and the Temple" to his list of themes in the fifth edition of his book (*The New Testament: A Student's Introduction*, 5th ed. [Boston: McGraw-Hill, 2006], 197).

4. Reddish, *Introduction to the Gospels*, 152.

- Characters who prophesy[5]
- Jesus and his apostles as prophets—like Elijah and Elisha, empowered by the same Spirit and ministering to Gentiles; like Moses, rejected twice by Jews[6]

I now had a list of fourteen themes. The list alone did not satisfy my curiosity, however. I was looking not only for Luke's themes but also for the reasons behind the themes, a likely backstory that might explain Luke's choices. Indeed, Luke does offer a kind of backstory. He wants his audience to "know the certainty of the things [they] have been taught" (Luke 1:4).[7] But to what "things" does he refer? Why would the Christians of his day need to "know the certainty of" them?

In order to answer these questions, I had to make sense of the fourteen themes. I began by consolidating them. Most of them seemed to be closely related. For example, the Holy Spirit, angels, the Scriptures, and characters who prophesy all have to do with God's plan of salvation. Through them, God speaks and acts to affirm that events like the Messiah's birth to a young woman from Nazareth and the conversion of the Roman centurion Cornelius are part of God's plan. Because Jesus is the agent of that plan, Luke calls him "Savior."

Other themes—the prominence of female characters; concern for sinners, the disabled, and the poor; inclusion of Gentiles; salvation of Samaritans; references to Elijah and Elisha; the centrality of Jerusalem—stress the universal scope of God's salvation. Early on, Luke affirms that Jesus rescues Abraham's descendants and saves sinners (Luke 1:68-79). He then cites prophecies that target other social groups. God anoints Jesus "to bring good news to the poor" (Luke 4:18; cf. Isa. 61:1). "The blind receive their sight, the lame walk, the lepers are cleansed, the deaf hear, the dead are raised" (Luke 7:22; cf. Isa. 35:5-6; 26:19). God pours out his Spirit "upon all flesh," "both men and women" (Acts 2:17-18; cf. Joel 2:28-29). God has set the apostles "to be a light for the Gentiles," to "bring salvation to the ends of the earth" (Acts 13:47; cf. Isa. 49:6). For Luke, "Everyone who calls on the name of the Lord shall be saved" (Acts 2:21; cf. Joel 2:32). Just as God sent Elijah to a Sidonian widow and Elisha to a

---

5. Luke Timothy Johnson, *The Writings of the New Testament: An Interpretation* (Philadelphia: Fortress Press, 1986), 205–8, 214.

6. Ibid., 208–11, 215–17, 222.

7. Unless otherwise indicated, all English New Testament quotations are taken from the NRSV. Since I agree with Donald Juel that "certainty" is a more accurate than "truth" as a rendering of *asphaleian*, this and other quotations of Luke 1:3-4 are from the NIV. See Juel, *Luke-Acts: The Promise of History* (Atlanta: John Knox, 1983), 15–16.

Syrian leper, God now sends Jesus and his witnesses to everyone from Jerusalem to Judea, Samaria, Asia Minor, Macedonia, Greece, and Rome.

Finally, the rejection of Jesus and his apostles—prophets like Moses—touches on the role of prayer, the presentation of Christianity as a legal religion, and (again) the centrality of Jerusalem. Jerusalem's leaders reject Jesus and his followers (e.g., Luke 13:33-34; 23:13-25; Acts 8:1; 21:10-14). Therefore, Jerusalem will suffer the consequence: the destruction of the temple (Luke 19:41-44). Meanwhile, Jesus and the apostles endure persecution. When they encounter opposition, they pray (Luke 22:39-46; Acts 4:31; 12:12; 16:25). When they are arrested, Roman officials pronounce them innocent (Luke 23:4-22; Acts 19:35-41; 26:31). Even if they are executed, they are never convicted of breaking Roman law.

Connecting these related themes yields a concise reconstruction of Luke's agenda:

- Jesus is the prophesied Messiah who, with his apostles, carries out God's plan of salvation through the forgiveness of sins. God confirms this by the intervention of angels, the prophecies of various characters, and the work of the Holy Spirit.
- Many Jews reject Jesus and the apostles as their ancestors rejected Moses. This is why the temple is destroyed.
- God's plan extends salvation to everyone: men and women; the poor and disabled; Jews, Samaritans, and Gentiles. It was already at work in the days of Elijah and Elisha; it now starts in Jerusalem and reaches to the ends of the earth.
- Christianity does not violate Roman law. If Christians are unjustly persecuted, they should pray.

The more I studied Luke-Acts, the better I liked this reconstruction. I especially liked the proposed parallels with the ministries of Elijah and Elisha and the rejection of Moses. I quickly noticed, however, that these are not the only potential prophetic models for Jesus and his apostles. There are several others. Samuel seems to set a pattern for Jesus' birth. Like Hosea, Zephaniah, Zechariah, Isaiah, Jeremiah, and Ezekiel, Jesus condemns the temple; like Jeremiah, he is falsely accused. Peter and Paul raise the dead as do Elijah and Elisha; John the Baptist is compared to Elijah and Samuel.

Now I had another long list: this time, a list of prophets who seem to shape Luke's story from beginning to end. I wanted to fit them into my consolidated outline of Luke's major themes. Some of them had already found a niche. Elijah and Elisha extend universal salvation; Moses suffers rejection by Jews. Still, why does Luke have Jesus pass the Holy Spirit to the apostles just as Elijah passed his spirit to Elisha? Why does he have Jesus condemn the temple in the words of Hosea, Zephaniah, Zechariah, Isaiah, Jeremiah, and Ezekiel? What about the parallels with Samuel's infancy narrative? Where does John the Baptist fit in? And how do Luke's themes and prophet parallels address the concerns of his original audience? I was eager to find out.

This book presents the results of my research. In chapter 1, I explain my thesis: that Luke portrays Jesus and his witnesses as prophets because Israel's prophets set a precedent for Gentile inclusion, Jewish rejection, and condemnation of the temple. In chapter 2, I present Luke's Jesus as the Messiah who saves sinners. In chapter 3, I show how parallels with Samuel establish Jesus and John as trustworthy prophets.

In chapters 4, 5, and 6, I focus on Luke's portrayal of Jesus. Like Elijah, Jesus resuscitates stricken children and appoints followers who will receive his spirit. Like Moses and Jeremiah, Jesus is rejected, arrested, and interrogated. Like Hosea, Zephaniah, Zechariah, Isaiah, Jeremiah, and Ezekiel, Jesus prophesies destruction for the holy city.

In chapters 7, 8, and 9, I turn the discussion to Acts. In scenes reminiscent of Elijah/Elisha stories, Peter and the apostles receive Jesus' spirit and perform Jesus' miracles. The Jerusalem council rejects them, however, just as they rejected Jesus—and just as Israel rejected Moses. Finally, starting with Philip and Peter and culminating with Paul, Spirit-filled prophets extend God's offer of salvation to Samaritans and Gentiles. In a brief conclusion, I examine some implications of my research for contemporary scholarship.

My investigation is based on five important assumptions. First, I concede that nobody knows for sure who wrote Luke-Acts. A second-century tradition asserts that Luke-Acts was the work of "Luke, the beloved physician" (Col. 4:14), but there is not enough first-century evidence to support this claim.[8] The author himself gives very little away. Although he describes himself with a masculine participle (Luke 1:3) and writes as if he were a traveling companion of Paul, he does not reveal his name.[9] He also neglects to specify his audience apart from dedications to his patron, Theophilus (Luke 1:1-4; Acts 1:1-2). If the anonymous author wrote for a particular Christian community, we have no idea who they were or where they lived. I call them "Luke" and "Luke's audience," but only because these designations are conventional and convenient.

---

8. For a summary of the evidence, see Beverly Roberts Gaventa, *The Acts of the Apostles*, ANTC (Nashville: Abingdon, 2003), 50.

9. Ibid.

Second, I agree with the scholarly consensus that Luke and Acts were written sometime during the 80s or 90s CE. This consensus is based partly on Luke's obvious concern for the fate of Jerusalem, expressed most clearly in Jesus' laments and prophecies (e.g., Luke 19:41-44; 21:20-24). They suggest a date soon after the Jewish War of 66–74 CE—a war that reached its climax in 70 CE with the Roman siege of Jerusalem and destruction of God's temple. Therefore, I am especially interested in how Luke's use of prophetic precedents addresses the concerns of Christians struggling to reinterpret their faith in the wake of that disaster.

Third, I subscribe to the Two-Source Theory, which postulates that Luke used two written sources when compiling his Gospel. One was a narrative composed around the time the temple was destroyed—a narrative now canonized as Mark's Gospel. The other was a collection of sayings attributed to Jesus and John the Baptist, compiled perhaps as early as the 50s and known to scholars as *Quelle* (Q). Although Q is now lost, its previous existence is attested by the large number of sayings that appear both in Luke and in Matthew.

That Luke probably copied from Mark and Q has important implications for interpreting his Gospel. In particular, we get some idea of how Luke addressed his audience's concerns by examining how he edited his sources. How did he adapt Mark and Q to his purposes? What did he convey by including episodes not found in Mark or Matthew? How does Luke convey his interpretation of Mark and Q by reiterating certain episodes and expressions in Luke as well as in Acts? I rely heavily on redaction criticism in order to answer these questions.[10]

Fourth, since many of my observations involve Luke's allusions to Israel's Scriptures, I use a strict method to justify detecting them. Although the allusions are by nature indirect, we can still identify them with some confidence. I use these five criteria to determine whether to give credence to a proposed allusion:

1. If neither author nor audience has access to the supposed referent, then the author does not allude to it.
2. The proposed allusion must correspond to its referent.
3. An author is much more likely to allude to a familiar text than to an obscure one.
4. An author often calls attention to allusions by emphasizing them in some way. Strategic placement of a proposed allusion thus adds to the evidence for its existence. The same holds for the repetition of important allusive words or congruent situations.

10. If I had identified Luke's source as Matthew, most of my conclusions would still stand.

5. An author will sometimes cite an important text more than once. Therefore, if a proposed allusion cites the referent of another confirmed citation, it was probably intended.

Two of these criteria are easily applied to Luke-Acts. For one, first-century Greek-speaking Christians had access to Greek Scriptures, usually in oral form. Luke, who claims to have been sponsored by a patron, might have referred to written copies.[11] For another, most (if not all) of those Scriptures were highly familiar to all but the newest Gentile converts. Israel's Scriptures shaped their imaginations. Many in Luke's audience had probably memorized large portions. It is the other three criteria—correspondence with a referent, rhetorical emphasis, and frequency of citation—that warrant careful consideration.

Once I have considered these criteria and identified Luke's allusions, four more criteria help me evaluate my interpretations:

1. The proposed allusion's interpretation must cohere with the author's established agenda.
2. The author's original audience must have been able to interpret the proposed allusion.
3. Other members of the author's extended audience—modern or premodern—should also recognize the proposed allusion and its interpretation.
4. The proposed allusion and its interpretation should be aesthetically pleasing and intellectually satisfying.[12]

Finally, I need to say a word about Luke's agenda. Issues like Jesus' messianic identity, Gentile inclusion, Jewish rejection, and the destruction of the temple,

---

11. It is impossible to tell which Greek version (or versions) Luke knew. The Greek text reproduced in this book is taken from Alfred Rahlfs, ed., *Septuaginta* (Stuttgart: Deutsche Bibelgesellschaft, 1979), checked against the variants noted in *Septuaginta: Vetus Testamentum graecum auctoritate Academiae Scientiarum Gottingensis editum* (Göttingen: Vandenhoeck & Ruprecht, 1931–). None of the variants suggests that Luke relied on a significantly different text. Unless otherwise indicated, all English quotations from Israel's Scriptures are my translation of that text. Septuagint vocabulary often differs significantly from the vocabulary of the Hebrew text translated in modern English versions. Chapter and verse numbers can differ as well. I follow the chapter and verse reckoning in the NRSV.

12. I have adapted these nine criteria from Richard B. Hays, who developed them for identifying Paul's allusions (*Echoes of Scripture in the Letters of Paul* [New Haven: Yale University Press, 1989], 29–32). Robert L. Brawley and Dennis R. MacDonald suggest similar criteria for identifying allusions in Luke-Acts (see Brawley, *Text to Text Pours Forth Speech: Voices of Scripture in Luke-Acts*, Indiana Studies in Biblical Literature 18 [Bloomington: Indiana University Press, 1995], 13–14; MacDonald, *Does the New Testament Imitate Homer? Four Cases from the Acts of the Apostles* [New Haven: Yale University Press, 2003], 2–7).

while critical for Luke's audience, seem somewhat obsolete and even offensive today. Luke's statements about Jewish rejection leading to the destruction of the temple make us uncomfortable—and rightly so. On the basis of such statements, Christians have accused Jews of Christ-killing; Christians have persecuted Jews in countless pogroms; Christians have stood by and even collaborated when Nazis imprisoned, tortured, and murdered millions of Jews during World War II.

For Luke's audience, the situation was quite different. They were not looking for occasions to persecute a Jewish minority. As a religious movement within Judaism, they themselves were a minority. Moreover, they were looking for answers. They believed that Jesus was the Messiah—the expected Davidic king—but their times did not seem like the expected messianic age. Why was the Messiah crucified? Why did his followers include so many Gentiles and so few Jews? Why was the temple destroyed? In this context, Luke's statements about Jewish rejection leading to the destruction of the temple probably seemed like a reasonable explanation.

I am indebted to many people for their inspiration and assistance in the making of this book. Thanks go first to my teachers. Donald Juel (whose wit and wisdom I have sorely missed these past ten years) trained me to recognize the concerns and biblical mind-set of the first Christians. Beverly Gaventa encouraged me to pursue this project when it was just a tantalizing idea. I am grateful to my students for thinking with me about Luke-Acts; to Albion College for the sabbatical leave in which I wrote the manuscript; to my colleagues Charlene McAfee Moss, Ellen Muehlberger, Jim Papandrea, Taylor Petrey, and Greg Smith for providing valuable feedback during the book's production.

Last but not least, I am grateful for the support of loving friends and family members. I could not live without them—especially my father and mother, to whom I dedicate this book.

LBarcode:

Copy: 1
Chron.:
Enum.:
Call No.: BS2589 .M440 2013
Author: McWhirter, Jocelyn.
Jocelyn McWhirter.
his witnesses in Luke-Acts /
Title: Rejected prophets : Jesus and

Due Date: 6/13/2020 04:30 PM

FBarcode:

ITEM CHARGED

1

The Role of Prophets in Luke-Acts

All four Gospels report that Jesus raised people from the dead. Together, they relate a total of three incidents. In Matt. 9:18-26, Mark 5:21-43, and Luke 8:40-56, Jesus restores a twelve-year-old girl to life. In John 11:1-44, he calls Lazarus out of the tomb. In Luke 7:11-17, he raises a widow's only son.

This third miracle, found only in Luke's Gospel, evokes the story of the prophet Elijah and the widow's son as told in 1 Kgs. 17:17-24. Luke seems to emphasize the connection by quoting 1 Kgs. 17:23: Jesus "gave him to his mother." He reinforces the parallel by indicating that it is not lost on the people of Nain. "A great prophet has risen among us," they exclaim (Luke 7:16).

The story of Jesus' raising the widow's son is just one example of Luke's clear and consistent effort to portray Jesus the Messiah as a prophet. Luke draws his concept of prophetic identity and mission from Israel's Scriptures.[1] A biblical prophet starts his or her career when the Lord comes to the prophet, perhaps through the Holy Spirit or in a vision. The prophet then speaks God's word to the people. Salvation oracles proclaim God's faithfulness to the covenants with Abraham and David; judgment oracles accuse the people of breaking the Mosaic covenant and pronounce sentence on them. Sometimes the prophet illustrates the oracle with a parable, a story that tricks its listeners into condemning themselves by inviting them to judge among its characters. At other times, the situation calls for a prophetic action, a stunt that drives home the prophet's point. Prophets often demonstrate their supernatural power by performing miracles, reading minds, and predicting the future.[2]

---

1. For other summaries of prophetic characteristics in Luke-Acts, see Paul S. Minear, *To Heal and to Reveal: The Prophetic Vocation According to Luke* (New York: Seabury, 1976), 87–90; Luke Timothy Johnson, *Luke-Acts: A Story of Prophet and People* (Chicago: Franciscan Herald, 1981), 25–26; David P. Moessner, *Lord of the Banquet: The Literary and Theological Significance of the Lukan Travel Narrative* (Minneapolis: Fortress Press, 1989), 48–50; Robert F. O'Toole, *Luke's Presentation of Jesus: A Christology*, SubBi 25 (Rome: Editrice Pontificio Istituto Biblico, 2004), 43–52.

2. For example, the "word of the Lord" comes to Jeremiah (Jer. 1:2, 4). Zechariah son of Jehoiada is possessed by the Holy Spirit (2 Chron. 24:20); Amos sees visions (Amos 7:1-9). Isaiah delivers a salvation

Luke lavishes these prophetic characteristics on Jesus, thereby distinguishing his work from the other canonical Gospels. This is not to say that the theme is absent from Matthew, Mark, and John. On the contrary, it is somewhat prominent in Mark. When Mark's Jesus gives offense in his hometown synagogue, for example, he compares himself to a dishonored prophet (Mark 6:4). Many believe that he is Elijah or one of the ancient prophets (Mark 6:15; 8:28). Like a prophet, he knows people's thoughts (Mark 2:8). He also foretells several events: his death, resurrection, and second coming (Mark 8:31; 9:31; 10:33-34; 13:24-28; 14:62); Judas's betrayal (Mark 14:18-21); the disciples' desertion (Mark 14:27-28); Peter's denial (Mark 14:30); the Jewish War of 66–74 (Mark 13:1-24). Ironically, Roman soldiers mock Jesus' prophetic ability even as a second cock-crow heralds the fulfillment of one of his prophecies (Mark 14:62-72).

Matthew also portrays Jesus as a prophet. Like Mark, he includes the dishonored prophet saying (Matt. 13:57), the mind reading (Matt. 9:4), predictions of future events (Matt. 16:21; 17:22-23; 20:18-28; 24:1-44; 26:20-25, 31-34, 64), and the fulfillment of the prophecy about Peter (Matt. 26:67-75). He includes one of Mark's sayings about Elijah and the ancient prophets, adding that some people also believe that Jesus is Jeremiah (Matt. 16:14). When he enters Jerusalem, the crowds hail him as a prophet (Matt. 21:11).[3] He implicitly compares his own execution to the murder of Israel's prophets (Matt. 23:29-36).

Even John's Gospel, with its focus on Jesus as the messianic Son whom God sends into the world, indicates that Jesus is a prophet. When John's Jesus recapitulates the Samaritan woman's marital history, she replies, "Sir, I see that you are a prophet" (John 4:19). Jesus never denies this. Soon afterward, on his return from Samaria to Galilee, he remarks that "a prophet has no honor in the prophet's own country" (John 4:44).

Luke, too, reports a version of the dishonored prophet saying (Luke 4:24). In addition, he includes the two Elijah sayings plus the mind-reading scenes and most of the other predictions found in Matthew and Mark.[4] This is consistent with the theory that Luke bases his narrative on Mark's story, interpolating

---

oracle in Isa. 2:1-4 and a judgment oracle in Isa. 1:1-20. Moses and Elijah perform miracles (Exod. 7:8-13; 1 Kgs. 18:30-39); Elisha reads his servant's mind (2 Kgs. 5:19-27); Micaiah predicts the future (1 Kgs. 22:5-23). Isaiah illustrates a judgment oracle by walking naked for three years (Isa. 20:1-6); Jeremiah, by smashing a clay pot (Jer. 19:1-13). Elijah and Elisha raise dead children (1 Kgs. 17:17-24; 2 Kgs. 4:32-37); Ahijah knows that Jeroboam's wife is pretending to be someone else (1 Kgs. 14:4-6); Samuel foretells Saul's encounters with three young men and a band of prophets (1 Sam. 10:3-6).

3. I am indebted to Charlene McAfee Moss for reminding me about this verse.

sayings from Q. As he edits Mark and Q, he retains most material that depicts Jesus as a prophet.

Luke does not stop there, however. He portrays a Spirit-filled Jesus who pronounces prophetic judgments, predictions, and supernatural insights not found in Mark or Q. What is more, Luke's Jesus often resembles one of Israel's prophets. His birth is similar to that of Samuel; he performs miracles like those of Elijah; he is rejected as were Moses and Jeremiah; he predicts the destruction of Jerusalem in the words of Hosea, Zechariah, Zephaniah, Isaiah, Jeremiah, and Ezekiel. All this leads other characters in Luke's narrative to recognize Jesus as a prophet.[5]

Moreover, Jesus is not the only prophet in Luke's two-volume work. Luke extends the motif to Jesus' forerunner John as well as to Jesus' followers—especially Peter and Paul—as portrayed in the Gospel's sequel, the book of Acts. According to Luke, those who bear witness to Jesus are prophets. They, too, are filled with the Holy Spirit. In the case of Peter and Paul, Jesus' Spirit is transferred to them just as the spirit of Elijah is transferred to his disciple Elisha. They experience prophetic calls, see prophetic visions, and pronounce prophetic judgments. Like Elijah and Elisha, they extend their ministry to Gentiles. And, like Moses and Jesus before them, they are rejected by their own people.

Luke thus makes it abundantly clear that Jesus and his witnesses are prophets just like the prophets in Israel's Scriptures. This has not been lost on New Testament scholars. Prophets and prophecy in Luke-Acts have attracted a good deal of interest over the last seventy years or so. From 1940 to 1957, commentators examined the parallels between Jesus and various biblical prophets. For example, Eric Burrows contemplated the Samuel parallels in Luke 1–2; P. Dabeck concentrated on Jesus' likeness to Elijah; C. H. Dodd laid out the allusions to Israel's prophets in Jesus' temple oracles; Howard Teeple explored Luke's portrayal of Jesus as a prophet like Moses.[6] Adrian

---

4. Luke 5:22; 9:8, 19, 22, 44; 11:47-51; 13:34-35; 18:31-33; 21:5-36; 22:21-22, 31-34. The exceptions include predictions at the Last Supper of the disciples' desertion (Mark 14:27-28; Matt. 26:31-32) and at Jesus' trial of the second coming (Mark 14:62; Matt. 26:64).

5. For other summaries of Jesus' prophetic activity in the four Gospels, see Gerhard Friedrich, "προφήτης," TDNT 6:841–48; Morna D. Hooker, The Signs of a Prophet: The Prophetic Actions of Jesus (Harrisburg, PA: Trinity Press International, 1997), 55–67.

6. Eric Burrows, "The Gospel of the Infancy: The Form of Luke Chapters 1 and 2," in The Gospel of the Infancy and Other Biblical Essays, The Bellarmine Series 6 (London: Burns Oates & Washbourne, 1940), 1–27; P. Dabeck, "Siehe, es erschienen Moses und Elias," Bib 23 (1942): 180–88; C. H. Dodd, "The Fall of Jerusalem and the 'Abomination of Desolation,'" JRS 37 (1947): 48–52; Howard M. Teeple, The Mosaic Eschatological Prophet (SBLMS 10; Philadelphia: Society of Biblical Literature, 1957), 86–88.

Hastings (1958) and Paul Minear (1976) then began the work of pulling these observations together. They concluded that Luke draws comparisons with Elijah and Moses in order to characterize Jesus as a prophet who ministers to Gentiles, brings God's salvation, and experiences rejection.[7] Minear extended the prophet designation to John the Baptist and the apostles.[8]

Others have continued their work. Starting in 1977, Luke Timothy Johnson began to sketch a portrait of Jesus and his witnesses as prophets like Elijah and Moses. They do what God's prophets have always done: extend salvation to Gentiles and get rejected by Jews.[9] David Tiede interpreted the Elijah and Moses parallels in light of Jesus' Jerusalem prophecies, understanding Gentile inclusion and Jewish rejection with respect to issues raised by the destruction of the temple.[10] Joel Green argued that Luke introduces parallels with Samuel, Elijah, Moses, and prophets who lament over Jerusalem in order to illustrate Jesus' place in salvation history.[11]

These and other scholars have not only explored the extent of prophets and prophecy in Luke-Acts but have also begun to address an important question. Why does Luke take a minor theme from his sources and embellish it, introducing elaborate allusions to the biblical prophets and then extending the theme through the Gospel narrative into its sequel in Acts? Why does Luke portray Jesus and his witnesses as prophets? For Odil Hannes Steck and David Moessner, prophetic parallels reiterate a Deuteronomistic pattern: God's people disobey; a prophet calls them to repentance; the people reject the prophet; God allows their enemies to prevail.[12] According to Johnson, the example of rejected prophets demonstrates God's faithfulness to a Gentile audience confused about

---

7. Adrian Hastings, *A Prophet and Witness in Jerusalem: A Study of the Teaching of Saint Luke* (London: Longmans, Green, and Co., 1958), 63–75; Minear, *To Heal and to Reveal*, 97–120.

8. Minear, *To Heal and to Reveal*, 82–96, 122–47.

9. Luke Timothy Johnson, *The Literary Function of Possessions in Luke-Acts*, SBLDS 39 (Missoula, MT: Scholars Press, 1977); Johnson, *Luke-Acts; The Gospel of Luke*, SP 3 (Collegeville, MN: Liturgical, 1991); Johnson, *The Acts of the Apostles*, SP 5 (Collegeville, MN: Liturgical, 1992); Johnson, "The Christology of Luke-Acts," in *Who Do You Say That I Am? Essays on Christology*, ed. Mark Allan Powell and David R. Bauer (Louisville: Westminster John Knox, 1999).

10. David L. Tiede, *Prophecy and History in Luke-Acts* (Philadelphia: Fortress Press, 1980).

11. Joel B. Green, *The Gospel of Luke*, NICNT (Grand Rapids: Eerdmans, 1997), 69, 381.

12. Odil Johannes Steck, *Israel und das gewaltsame Geschick der Propheten: Untersuchung zur Überlieferung des deuteronomistischen Geschichtsbildes im Alten Testament, Spätjudentum und Urchristentum*, WMANT 23 (Neukirchen-Vluyn: Neukirchener, 1967), 63–64; David Moessner, "Paul and the Pattern of the Prophet Like Moses in Acts," in *SBL 1983 Seminar Papers*, ed. Kent H. Richards, SBLSP 22 (Chico, CA: Scholars Press, 1983), 206; Moessner, "The Christ Must Suffer: New Light on the Jesus–Peter, Stephen, Paul Parallels in Luke-Acts," *NovT* 28 (1986): 246–47; Moessner, *Lord of the Banquet*, 84.

Jewish unbelief.[13] Green agrees with Craig Evans and Robert O'Toole: Luke's prophet parallels portray Jesus as the Messiah who brings salvation.[14] Thomas Brodie theorizes that the text of Luke-Acts is based on a prototype that patterns Jesus' story on the Elijah-Elisha narrative.[15] J. Severino Croatto argues that parallels with Elijah illustrate Jesus' healing miracles while parallels with Moses illustrate his teaching.[16]

I take a somewhat different view. As I see it, the portrayal of Jesus and his witnesses as prophets constitutes an important part of Luke's overall agenda: to assure his audience of "the certainty of the things [they] have been taught" (Luke 1:4). Although they have received Christian instruction, Luke's audience seems to be questioning some of its central claims.[17] This is perhaps understandable, as their times did not much resemble the expected messianic age. They believed that the messianic age had been inaugurated with the advent of Jesus the Messiah, the Anointed One eagerly awaited by many first-century Jews. Most Jews, however, were not expecting a messiah like Jesus. They were looking for a Davidic king who would conquer his Gentile enemies (in their case, the Romans) and rule in Jerusalem.

The foundation for these expectations lies in 2 Samuel 7. Here the prophet Nathan explains to King David that God will establish the kingdom of David's "offspring" forever (2 Sam. 7:12-13, 16).[18] "He shall build a house for my name," says God, referring to the temple (2 Sam. 7:13). "I will be a father to him, and he shall be a son to me" (2 Sam. 7:14). Other Scriptures pick up the motif. Psalm 2, for example, depicts a king enthroned by God in Jerusalem. The psalm identifies this king as the Lord's "anointed," to whom God decrees, "You are my son; today I have begotten you" (Ps. 2:2, 7). Although the Gentiles conspire against

13. Johnson, *Literary Function of Possessions*, 122; Johnson, *Luke-Acts*, 21.

14. Craig A. Evans, "Luke's Use of the Elijah/Elisha Narratives and the Ethics of Election," *JBL* 106 (1987): 77; Robert O'Toole, "The Parallels between Jesus and Moses," *BTB* 20 (1990): 28; O'Toole, *Luke's Presentation of Jesus*, 52; Green, *Gospel of Luke*, 69, 381.

15. Thomas L. Brodie, *Luke the Literary Interpreter: Luke-Acts as a Systematic Rewriting and Updating of the Elijah-Elisha Narrative in 1 and 2 Kings* (Rome: Pontifical University of St. Thomas Aquinas, 1988); Brodie, *Proto-Luke: The Oldest Gospel Account: A Christ-Centered Synthesis of Old Testament History Modelled Especially on the Elijah-Elisha Narrative* (Limerick: Dominical Biblical Institute, 2006).

16. J. Severino Croatto, "Jesus, Prophet Like Elijah, and Prophet-Teacher Like Moses in Luke-Acts," *JBL* 124, no. 3 (2005): 461.

17. Donald Juel, *Luke-Acts: The Promise of History* (Atlanta: John Knox, 1983), 15–16; Robert C. Tannehill, *The Narrative Unity of Luke-Acts: A Literary Interpretation* (Philadelphia: Fortress Press, 1986), 1:12; Richard I. Pervo, *Acts: A Commentary*, Hermeneia (Minneapolis: Fortress Press, 2008), 22; John T. Carroll, *Luke: A Commentary*, NTL (Louisville: Westminster John Knox, 2012), 6.

18. The following quotations from 2 Sam. 7, Ps. 2, and Isa. 11 are NRSV translations.

God's king, he will subdue them. He will "break them with a rod of iron, and dash them in pieces like a potter's vessel" (Ps. 2:9). A third prophecy about a coming king is found in Isaiah 11. It concerns "a shoot . . . from the stump of Jesse"—that is, a descendant of Jesse's son David (Isa. 11:1). "The spirit of the Lord shall rest on him," making him a righteous judge (Isa. 11:2-5). He will gather dispersed Jews, cease hostilities with northern Israelites, and rule over a peaceable kingdom (Isa. 11:6-12).

By 63 BCE, when Pompey's Roman legions marched into Jerusalem, these prophecies had yet to be fulfilled. David's progeny had indeed ruled for many generations after his death. His dynasty had come to an end, however, with the Babylonian conquest in 587 BCE. Since then, Jerusalem had been under the sway of several successive Gentile powers: Babylonians, Persians, Alexander the Great, Ptolemies, Seleucids. Starting with the Maccabean Revolt in 167 BCE, Jews had enjoyed some measure of independence and home rule. Their Hasmonean leaders, however, were most certainly not Davidic kings. Now, with the Romans in charge, it seemed high time for God to send the Messiah.

Much messianic expectation before 70 CE was based on prophecies like 2 Sam. 7:12-14; Psalm 2; and Isa. 11:1-12, if extant Jewish literature is any indication.[19] Perhaps the best example is found in the *Psalms of Solomon*. This noncanonical collection of Jewish psalms seems to reflect anti-Roman sentiment in the wake of Pompey's invasion. It therefore includes two psalms about the coming Messiah, one of which alludes to all three prophecies (*Pss. Sol.* 17–18).[20] Wielding "an iron rod" and "the word of his mouth," the "son of David" will "destroy the unlawful nations" and place them "under his yoke" (*Pss. Sol.* 17:24, 30).[21] He will "purge Jerusalem," rallying righteous Jews and restoring the holy city to its original splendor (*Pss. Sol.* 17:22, 26, 30-31). The "Lord Messiah" will then rule as a righteous king and a wise judge (*Pss. Sol.* 17:26-29, 32). Such was the vision for the messianic age.

Luke's Christian audience, probably living in the 80s CE, was experiencing a very different scenario. Their Messiah, Jesus, was no warrior. He had not led a Jewish army to defeat the Romans. He was an artisan from Nazareth whom the Romans had crucified. Some of his most prominent followers, including Peter and Paul, had already shared his fate. Most Jews—especially Pharisees—rejected

---

19. See, e.g., 4QFlor; 4QpIsa ᵃ8–10 III, 11–25; 1Q28b V, 24–46; *1 Enoch* 48:8; 49:3; 62:3, 8; *T. Levi* 18:5; 7; *T. Judah* 24:6.

20. *Pss. Sol.* 17–18.

21. Quotations of the *Psalms of Solomon* are taken from the translation by Robert Wright (*OTP* 2:651–70).

Christian claims, while many Samaritans and even uncircumcised Gentiles had become Jesus' followers. Moreover, Jerusalem and its temple had not been restored by the Messiah. They had been destroyed by the Romans.[22]

"An Orderly Account"

Luke's story focuses on these anomalies. He highlights them by using various characters to raise the relevant issues. John the Baptist, a crucified criminal, a disciple named Cleopas, and various apostles all voice questions about Jesus' messianic identity and mission. Pharisees accuse Jesus of blasphemy and doubt his ability to forgive sins. The disciples, an Ethiopian eunuch, and Peter wonder about Samaritan and Gentile inclusion, while Jesus himself puzzles over Jewish rejection. When bystanders admire the beautiful temple, one can almost hear Luke's audience mourning their loss.

In order to explain the anomalies, Luke uses three basic strategies—strategies that will shape our discussion in the following chapters. First, he structures his "orderly account" (Luke 1:3) around the Messiah's death, acceptance by Samaritans and Gentiles, rejection by Jews, and activity in the Holy City. He introduces these motifs right away. The story begins in and around Jerusalem with the birth of Jesus, acclaimed as the Messiah who will save his people from their sins. Even as the prophet Simeon announces the advent of God's salvation, he foreshadows Gentile inclusion, Jewish rejection, and Jesus' crucifixion.

Themes of a crucified Messiah, salvation from sins, Jewish rejection, Gentile inclusion, and Jerusalem continue to shape Luke's story of Jesus' ministry in Galilee (Luke 4:14—9:50). The sermon in Nazareth—his first public act—involves an implied messianic claim, a foreshadowing of Gentile inclusion, and rejection in his own hometown. True to his mission "to bring good news to the poor" (Luke 4:18; cf. Isa. 61:1), Jesus ministers to the disabled. To fulfill Joel's prophecy about God's salvation for "young" and "old," "both men and women" (Acts 2:17-21; cf. Joel 2:28-32), he heals boys, girls, men, and women, all the while gathering male and female followers. He stays away from Gentiles. He does, however, minister to unclean Jews, forgiving sinners and associating with tax collectors. This raises the hackles of scribes and Pharisees. Near the end of Jesus' time in Galilee, Peter declares that Jesus is the Messiah. Jesus' response: the Jerusalem elders, chief priests, and scribes will reject him and kill him.

Jesus' Galilean ministry is followed by a long journey to Jerusalem (Luke 9:51—19:44)—a journey that he knows will lead to the cross. On the way,

---

22. Juel, *Luke-Acts*, 117–20.

Jesus continues his ministry to disabled people (male and female), tax collectors, and sinners. This leads to more conflict with Jewish leaders. Luke punctuates the journey with two laments over the holy city. In the first, Jesus identifies Jerusalem as "the city that kills the prophets" (Luke 13:34); in the second, he foretells the coming devastation.

When Jesus finally enters the temple (Luke 19:45), the conflict comes to a head. Jerusalem's religious leaders have Jesus sentenced to death. As he dies, he saves one last sinner. God raises Jesus from the dead, but the religious leaders reject the eyewitness testimony of Peter and the apostles. The Gospel then spreads from Jerusalem to Judea, Samaria, and the ends of the earth, leading to the inclusion of Samaritans and Gentiles. The result: more Jewish rejection.

Luke supports this "orderly account" with a second narrative strategy: the frequent introduction of God's own testimony. Sometimes God speaks through heavenly messengers, the angels who announce Jesus' birth and instruct the apostles. God's written word consistently testifies to God's ongoing work of salvation. Often, God speaks through characters who prophesy and see visions. Nine times, God acts directly through the Holy Spirit. Twice, a voice from heaven is heard. In these ways, Luke affirms that a crucified Messiah, salvation for sinners, Jewish rejection, Gentile inclusion, and the destruction of the temple have always been part of God's plan.[23]

Third, and most importantly for our purposes, Luke characterizes Jesus and his witnesses as prophets. He thus reminds his audience of the precedents set by the biblical prophets—prophets like Samuel, Moses, Elijah, Elisha, Hosea, Zephaniah, Zechariah, Isaiah, Jeremiah, and Ezekiel. They were sent to Gentiles; they were consistently rejected in Israel; they foretold enemy invasions brought on by Israel's disobedience. Therefore, first-century Christians should not be surprised at acceptance by Gentiles, opposition from Jews, and the loss of the temple. Even though their times do not much resemble the expected messianic age, they do look remarkably like the age of the prophets.

"So That You May Know the Certainty"

An author's skeptical audience; his need to legitimate his protagonists; his use of prophets to set precedents for them: this comprehensive theory about Luke's agenda rests largely on circumstantial evidence. Luke wants his audience to know with certainty. He is indisputably preoccupied with Gentile inclusion,

---

23. Henry J. Cadbury, *The Making of Luke-Acts*, 3rd ed. (Peabody, MA: Hendrickson, 1999), 34–40, 301–8; Brigid Curtin Frein, "Narrative Predictions, Old Testament Prophecies and Luke's Sense of Fulfillment," *NTS* 40 (1994): 22–37.

Jewish rejection, and the temple. He likens his protagonists to prophets, mostly by implication, and the activities of those prophets cohere with his major themes. The theory is a likely explanation for all this internal evidence. Still, is there any outside evidence that might support it?

There is indeed. The strategy of using biblical heroes as precedents for protagonists was not invented by Luke. It is also favored by at least one other ancient historiographer: the anonymous author of 1 Maccabees, written about two hundred years before Luke-Acts. First Maccabees relates the history of the Maccabean Revolt (164–167 BCE) led by the priest Mattathias and his sons Judas "Maccabeus," Jonathan, and Simon against the Seleucid king Antiochus IV. It recounts how the victorious brothers consolidated their power when Antiochus's son Alexander appointed Jonathan to the high priesthood (1 Macc. 10:18-21). Upon Jonathan's death, his brother Simon succeeded him in that office. In addition, Simon acted as governor and ethnarch, thus uniting religious and political leadership in one ruler (1 Macc. 14:35-49). The story ends with the death of Simon and the succession of his son John Hyrcanus—that is, with the establishment of the Hasmonean dynasty that governed Jerusalem until Pompey's invasion in 63 BCE (1 Macc. 16:23-24).

Although the Hasmoneans instituted self-rule in Jerusalem for the first time since the Babylonian conquest in 587 BCE, many Jews opposed them. Some never accepted their claim to the high priesthood. The Hasmoneans, after all, were not a high priestly family. Even more offensive were the royal trappings they assumed. Their authority in the temple, their control of Jerusalem, their purple garments and gold ornaments—all seemed like a bid for power by a family of upstart priests from Modein.[24]

Writing sometime during or shortly after the reign of John Hyrcanus (134–104 BCE), the author of 1 Maccabees champions the Hasmonean rulers and seeks to legitimate their authority. He therefore portrays Mattathias and his sons as heroes of the revolution; defenders of the law who rescued Jerusalem from the profanities of the Gentiles. To this end, he draws comparisons, both implicit and explicit, between his protagonists and biblical heroes who kept God's law in the face of opposition, even at the risk of their own lives.

The author first deploys this strategy when describing the initial act of rebellion in which Mattathias assassinates a Jew about to sacrifice to Gentile gods (1 Macc. 2:23-26). He likens the zeal of Mattathias to that of his priestly ancestor Phinehas, a grandson of Aaron who murdered an Israelite for defying God's command by marrying a Gentile woman (Num. 25:6-9). God rewards

---

24. For arguments about the political nature of 1 Maccabees, see David A. deSilva, *Introducing the Apocrypha: Message, Content, and Significance* (Grand Rapids: Baker Academic, 2002), 249–50.

Phinehas with "a covenant of perpetual priesthood" "for him and his descendants after him" (Num. 25:13). The implication of this parallel for Mattathias and his descendants is obvious.

The author goes on to make further comparisons with other Israelite heroes. The initial stages of the rebellion evoke David's sojourn in the Judean wilderness, while the battles of Judas Maccabeus resemble the battles of Saul's son Jonathan (1 Macc. 2:29-30, 42-43; 3:18-19; 5:40-41; cf. 1 Sam. 22:1-2; 23:14; 14:6, 8). As he prays for victory, Judas explicitly invokes the God of David and Jonathan (1 Macc. 4:30). Finally, in his deathbed speech to his sons, Mattathias mentions several of Israel's heroes. Each was faithful to God and the law. Accordingly, each was rewarded: Abraham with righteousness; Joseph, Joshua, and David with rule; Phinehas with "the covenant of everlasting priesthood" (1 Macc. 2:54); Caleb with land; Elijah with heaven; Hanaiah, Azariah, Mishael, and Daniel with salvation from execution by Gentiles.[25] If Judas, Jonathan, and Simon display similar zeal, presumably they will receive similar rewards (1 Macc. 2:51-64).[26]

In the end, of course, they do. "How shall we thank Simon and his sons?" ask the Jewish people. "For he and his brothers and the house of his father have stood firm; they have fought and repulsed Israel's enemies and established its freedom" (1 Macc. 14:25-26). Anyone persuaded by parallels with Israel's heroes has a ready answer: Simon and his sons should be rewarded with high priesthood and royal power.

Why does the author of 1 Maccabees draw these parallels? It would seem that he addresses a skeptical audience. They are torn between the claims of their high-priestly rulers and the criticisms of the opposition party. Therefore, in order to legitimate the Hasmonean dynasty, the author of 1 Maccabees compares them to biblical heroes—mainly priests and rulers—who kept God's law, saved Israel from Gentile oppressors, and were rewarded with power and authority. As David deSilva puts it, "The choice of intertexture . . . makes the implicit, yet unmistakable, claim that the Hasmonean household's occupation of the high priesthood and the de facto leadership of Israel . . . is a legitimate one, the family having risen to that status in precisely the same way as had Phinehas and David: through zeal for the law and through military virtuosity."[27]

Similarly, Luke's choice of intertexture makes the claim that Jesus and his witnesses, even though they have not yet brought about the expected messianic

---

25. Quotations from 1 Maccabees are taken from the NRSV.

26. Daniel J. Harrington, "1 Maccabees," in *The HarperCollins Study Bible*, ed. Harold W. Attridge, rev. ed. (San Francisco: HarperSanFrancisco, 2006), 1484.

27. DeSilva, *Introducing the Apocrypha*, 259–60.

age, are nonetheless carrying out God's purposes. Like Israel's prophets before them, sent by God and full of the Holy Spirit, they extend God's offer of universal salvation, prophesy against Jerusalem, and meet with resistance from their fellow Jews. Luke thus assures his skeptical audience that the Christian message of a rejected messiah who saves both Jews and Gentiles is in fact the truth, and that even the unexpected destruction of Jerusalem is part of God's plan.

2

Messiah and Savior

Prophetic precedents cannot address the chief objection to early Christian faith: its central claim that Jesus, a condemned and crucified criminal, is actually the prophesied Messiah. Judging from the vocabulary of his purpose statement, Luke seeks above all to answer this objection. "I too decided . . . to write an orderly account for you," he tells his audience, "so that you may know [*epignōs*] the certainty [*asphaleian*] of the things you have been taught" (Luke 1:3-4). Luke reiterates this vocabulary once more at the beginning of Acts: "Let the entire house of Israel know [*ginōsketo*] with certainty [*asphalōs*] that God has made him both Lord and Christ, this Jesus whom you crucified" (Acts 2:36).[1] Above all, his audience needs assurance that Jesus is the Messiah.

Unfortunately for Luke, however, no prophet sets a precedent for being God's anointed king. Luke needs other strategies to bolster this particular claim. Since those strategies create a context for Luke's use of prophetic precedents, we need to examine them here. We will find that Luke demonstrates Jesus' messianic identity in the same ways that he shows how Gentile inclusion, Jewish rejection, and the destruction of the temple are part of God's plan for the messianic age. He structures his narrative around it, using various characters to voice the concerns of his audience. He follows his written sources Mark and Q, especially when they cite messianic prophecy—prophecy that in Luke's judgment refers to the Messiah. He then supplements his sources with God's testimony through additional messianic prophecies, angels, characters who prophesy, and the Holy Spirit. He uses every possible means to convince his audience of this indispensable "certainty."

Explicating Jesus' messianic identity is only half the job. Luke must also delineate Jesus' messianic mission. Clearly, Jesus had not conquered the Romans. He was not ruling in Jerusalem. How then was he supposed to have saved Israel? Jesus saves by forgiving sins, says Luke. A Spirit-inspired prophet announces this. The Scriptures confirm it. Luke's narrative portrays a Jesus who

---

1. See also Beverly Roberts Gaventa, *The Acts of the Apostles*, ANTC (Nashville: Abingdon, 2003), 79.

forgives sinners from his first miracles in Galilee to his death on Calvary. He cannot follow a prophetic precedent because no prophet claims to forgive sin. That prerogative is reserved for God alone. Luke's Jesus claims that prerogative, however, and more than once he supports his claim by acting like a prophet. Surely a man who tells parables, reads minds, and predicts the future must speak for God when he says, "Your sins are forgiven you."

"The Messiah Is Jesus"

Luke's emphasis on Jesus as the Messiah is based on a similar emphasis in Mark and Q. Luke therefore reproduces several episodes where his sources appeal to messianic prophecies. He agrees with Mark about the heavenly proclamation at Jesus' baptism: "You are my Son" (Luke 3:22//Mark 1:11). This statement identifies Jesus as the Messiah, God's "son" according to 2 Sam. 7:14 and Ps. 2:7. Luke repeats the Q story about a query from John the Baptist: "Are you the one who is to come?" (Luke 7:19). Jesus answers by confirming his messianic identity with allusions to Isa. 26:19; 35:5-6; 61:1: "Go and tell John what you have seen and heard: the blind receive their sight, the lame walk, the lepers are cleansed, the deaf hear, the dead are raised, and the poor have good news brought to them" (Luke 7:18-23//Matt. 11:2-6). Further prophecies are adapted from Mark. After accepting Peter's confession that he is "the Messiah of God" (Luke 9:20//Mark 8:29), Jesus is transfigured. He radiates messianic glory as the heavenly voice reaffirms, "This is my Son" (Luke 9:35//Mark 9:7). When Jesus finally enters Jerusalem, the scene evokes Zech. 9:9: "Lo, your king comes to you . . . mounted on a donkey." The people acclaim him in the words of Ps. 118:26: "Blessed is the king who comes in the name of the Lord" (Luke 19:28-40//Mark 11:1-10). At his trial, Jesus finally admits that he is "the Messiah," the "Son of God," citing Dan. 7:13 and Ps. 110:1 to describe the "Son of Man seated at the right hand of the power of God" (Luke 22:67-70//Mark 14:61-62).

Luke not only relies on his sources for messianic prophecies but also reiterates prophecies that focus on the necessity of the crucifixion. Three times in Mark's Gospel, Jesus affirms that his mission involves suffering, rejection, execution, and resurrection (Luke 9:22, 44; 18:31-33//Mark 8:31; 9:31; 10:33-34). While teaching in the temple, Jesus cites Ps. 118:22 to illustrate his fate: "The stone that the builders rejected has become the cornerstone" (Luke 20:17//Mark 12:10). The night before he dies, Jesus tells his disciples that he "is going as it has been determined" (Luke 22:22//Mark 14:21). Here Luke alters Mark's phrase "as it is written of him," adding a bit more stress on God's preordained plan. All this is borne out in the passion narrative with its ironic placard "This is the King of the Jews" (Luke 23:38//Mark 15:26) and its allusions to Davidic psalms about tormentors dividing their victim's clothes and offering him sour wine (Luke 23:34//Mark 15:24; Luke 23:36//Mark 15:36; cf. Pss. 22:18; 69:21).

Luke's sources make a strong case that the crucified Jesus is the prophesied Messiah—but apparently Luke needs a stronger one. He gets it by augmenting God's testimony in Mark and Q with additional messianic prophecies. He also brings in angels, characters who prophesy, and the Holy Spirit. According to Luke, God proclaims Jesus' messianic identity even before his conception when the angel Gabriel describes him as "the Son of the Most High," the one who will inherit David's throne and "reign over the house of Jacob forever" (Luke 1:32-33). This is confirmed by three Spirit-filled prophets: John the Baptist (in utero), his mother Elizabeth, and his father Zechariah (Luke 1:41-44, 76). When Jesus is born in Bethlehem, "the city of David," angels announce the advent of "a Savior, who is the Messiah, the Lord" (Luke 2:11). Prompted by the Holy Spirit, Simeon recognizes Jesus as "the Lord's Messiah" (Luke 2:25-32). Jesus' first public act is the preaching of a sermon based on Isa. 61:1-2, a prophecy that outlines the mission of one "anointed" by God (Luke 4:16-21). The third time Jesus predicts his suffering and death, Luke adds to Mark's account that "everything that is written about the Son of Man by the prophets will be accomplished" (Luke 18:31).[2]

After these predictions come to pass, Luke tells how one of Jesus' disciples expresses some serious doubts. That disciple is Cleopas, one of two disciples who meet the risen Jesus on the road to Emmaus (Luke 24:13-35). Not recognizing his fellow traveler, Cleopas summarizes the situation so far. He relates "the things about Jesus of Nazareth, a prophet mighty in deed and word, and how our chief priests and leaders handed him over to be condemned to death and crucified him." He then explains the source of his confusion: "But we had hoped that he was the one to redeem Israel" (Luke 24:19-21).

Cleopas conveys the sentiments of Luke's audience. He knows that Israel's Scriptures never indicate that the Messiah will suffer a humiliating execution. His confusion is understandable. Nevertheless, it draws a stunning rebuke from Luke's Jesus: "'Oh, how foolish you are, and how slow of heart to believe all that the prophets have declared! Was it not necessary that the Messiah should suffer these things and then enter into his glory?' Then beginning with Moses and all the prophets, he interpreted to them the things about himself in the scriptures" (Luke 24:25-27). Jesus later repeats the catechesis, this time with "the eleven and their companions" (Luke 24:33). He demonstrates that the Scriptures indeed

---

2. The clause is missing from Mark 10:33-34.

prophesy "that the Messiah is to suffer and to rise from the dead on the third day" (Luke 24:44-46).[3] Peter reiterates this important statement in Acts 3:18; Paul makes a similar affirmation in Acts 24:14-15.

Unfortunately, it is hard to tell which Scriptures Jesus has in mind. He cites only one relevant passage. The night before he dies, he tells his disciples, "This scripture must be fulfilled in me, 'And he was counted among the lawless'; and indeed what is written about me is being fulfilled" (Luke 22:37; cf. Isa. 53:12). Other citations in Luke-Acts round out Luke's collection of Scriptures that are now being fulfilled. For example, Luke's Gospel mentions three royal prophecies, all from the Psalms:

> Blessed is the king
> > who comes in the name of the Lord! (Luke 19:38//Mark 11:9-10; cf. Ps. 118:26)

> The stone that the builders rejected has become the cornerstone. (Luke 20:17//Mark 12:10-11; cf. Ps. 118:22)

> The Lord said to my Lord,
> > "Sit at my right hand,
> > until I make your enemies your footstool." (Luke 20:42-43//Mark 12:36; cf. Ps. 110:1)[4]

In Acts, Luke supplements these three prophecies with several others.[5] Most are placed in Peter's and Paul's speeches—speeches that show how Jesus' followers continued to proclaim him as the Messiah, crucified and raised from the dead. According to Luke, sometimes they supported their claims with passages from Israel's Scriptures.

Peter cites three relevant prophecies in two of his speeches: one to the crowd of pilgrims at Pentecost and the other before an assembly of Jerusalem's rulers, elders, and scribes (Acts 2:14-36; 4:5-12). In both speeches, he stresses that the crucified and risen Jesus is in fact the Messiah, handed over "according to the definite plan and foreknowledge of God" (Acts 2:23).[6] He then quotes

---

3. David L. Tiede also stresses the importance of Jesus' conversations with Cleopas and the twelve (*Prophecy and History in Luke-Acts* [Philadelphia: Fortress Press, 1980], 99).

4. Robert C. Tannehill, *The Narrative Unity of Luke-Acts: A Literary Interpretation* (Philadelphia: Fortress Press, 1986), 1:194.

5. See also ibid., 1:285–86.

6. See also Acts 2:36; 4:10.

verses from three psalms. One is Ps. 110:1; another, Ps. 118:22 (Acts 2:34-35; 4:11). To these verses, already cited in Luke's Gospel, he adds a third:

> He was not abandoned to Hades,
>> nor did his flesh experience corruption. (Acts 2:31; cf. Ps. 16:10)[7]

Together, the three verses show that David, identified as a prophet in Acts 2:30, spoke of the Messiah's death, resurrection, and ascension.

After Peter's first arrest, Luke introduces a novel interpretation of Psalm 2, the psalm that envisions the Lord's "anointed" as a "king" who will "break [the nations] with a rod of iron, and dash them in pieces like a potter's vessel." In their prayer for boldness in the face of persecution, the believers quote verses 1-2:

> Why did the Gentiles rage,
>> and the peoples imagine vain things?
> The kings of the earth took their stand,
>> and the rulers have gathered together
>>> against the Lord and against his Messiah. (Acts 4:25-26)

At first glance, the "peoples," "kings," and "rulers" seem to represent Gentiles who oppose the Jewish king. For Peter's friends, however, Ps. 2:1-2 predicts Jesus' trials. The "king" is Herod Antipas, the "ruler" is Pontius Pilate, and the "peoples" are "the Gentiles and the people of Israel, gathered together against Jesus, whom [the Lord] anointed" (Acts 4:27). Significantly, Peter's friends recognize that these enemies of Jesus intended only "whatever [God's] hand and [God's] plan had predestined to take place" (Acts 4:28). It was God's intention all along that the Messiah should be crucified, and even Psalm 2—a prophecy about the Messiah's victory over his Gentile enemies—testifies to that fact.

Once opposition to the apostles reaches its climax with the stoning of Stephen, the good news begins to spread outside Jerusalem. Philip proclaims the Messiah in Samaria (Acts 8:1-13). Then, on the road from Jerusalem to Gaza, he encounters an Ethiopian sitting in his chariot, reading Isa. 53:7-8:

> Like a sheep he was led to the slaughter
>> and like a lamb silent before its shearer,
>> so he does not open his mouth.

---

7. For more on Luke's use of Pss. 16 and 110 see Tiede, *Prophecy and History*, 102; Donald Juel, *Luke-Acts: The Promise of History* (Atlanta: John Knox, 1983), 61.

> In his humiliation justice was denied him.
>> Who can describe his generation?
>>> For his life is taken away from the earth. (Acts 8:32-33)

Presumably, the prophecy foretells Jesus' crucifixion. Philip confirms this. "Starting with this scripture, he proclaimed to [the Ethiopian] the good news about Jesus" (Acts 8:35).

Finally, Paul brings the message with its scriptural underpinnings to Asia Minor, Macedonia, Achaia, and Italy. His inaugural sermon in the synagogue at Pisidian Antioch cites Ps. 2:7; Isa. 55:3; and Ps. 16:10:

> You are my Son,
>> today I have begotten you. (Acts 13:33)
>> I will give you the holy promises made to David. (Acts 13:34)
>> You will not let your Holy One experience corruption. (Acts 13:35)

Together, these three citations support Paul's contention that God raised the Messiah from the dead.

These are the last such citations in Luke-Acts, even though Paul continues to "declare the whole purpose of God" for another fifteen chapters (Acts 20:27). From Pisidian Antioch, he goes on to the synagogue at Thessalonica. There, he argues "from the Scriptures, explaining and proving that it was necessary for the Messiah to suffer and to rise from the dead, and saying, 'This is the Messiah, Jesus whom I am proclaiming to you'" (Acts 17:2-3). He does the same in Corinth (Acts 18:4-5), together with Priscilla and Aquila, who later teach Apollos to show "by the scriptures that the Messiah is Jesus" (Acts 18:28). His defense before Festus and King Agrippa includes the assertion that he has said "nothing but what the prophets and Moses said would take place: that the Messiah must suffer" (Acts 26:22-23).[8] Acts closes with Paul in Rome, "testifying to the kingdom of God and trying to convince [Jews] about Jesus from the law of Moses and from the prophets" (Acts 28:23). In these final episodes, Luke does not specify Paul's references. Nevertheless, we can imagine that he cites verses about Jesus the Son of David and Son of God, rejected, tried, executed, raised, and exalted to God's right hand—verses like Pss. 2:1-2, 7; 16:10; 110:1; 118:22; and Isa. 53:7-8, 12; 55:3.

---

8. Tiede, *Prophecy and History*, 99.

"This Fellow Welcomes Sinners"

Luke's argument about a crucified messiah raises important questions about the Messiah's mission. In his day, the Romans were still in control. The temple was in ruins. Things seemed worse than Jesus had left them. Nevertheless, Luke affirms that the Messiah came to save Israel. He begins with the story of Zechariah and his Spirit-inspired prophecy that God "has raised up a mighty savior" from David's line, as God "spoke through the mouth of his holy prophets" (Luke 1:69-70). Not only does Zechariah proclaim the Messiah's advent, but he also describes the Messiah's mission: to fulfill God's promises to save God's people from their enemies (Luke 1:71, 73). For Luke, the redemption of Israel means rescue from enemies—but with an unexpected twist. According to Zechariah, John will prepare the Messiah's way not by inciting revolution but by giving "knowledge of salvation to his people by the forgiveness of their sins" (Luke 1:77).

Luke's Jesus consistently fulfills Zechariah's prophecy. From the beginning of his ministry through his crucifixion, Jesus concentrates on saving sinners.[9] He starts in two episodes borrowed from Mark by forgiving the sins of a paralytic (whom he then heals) and eating with tax collectors and sinners at Levi's house (Luke 5:17-32//Mark 2:1-17). In both instances, he meets with opposition from attendant Pharisees. "Who is this who is speaking blasphemies?" they ask. "Who can forgive sins but God alone?" (Luke 5:21//Mark 2:7). "Why do you eat and drink with tax collectors and sinners?" (Luke 5:30//Mark 2:16). Undoubtedly, the first Christians were peppered with questions like these. They reflect the immediate concerns of Luke's audience.

In answer, Luke stresses that Jesus can and does forgive sins. He builds on the two Mark stories with four additional "forgiven sinner" episodes. Each episode includes characters who somehow question Jesus' mission to sinners. Luke counters their objections by emphasizing the divine impetus behind Jesus' mission. In two instances, Jesus fulfills prophecies. In the other two, Jesus acts like a prophet. This assures Luke's audience that forgiveness lies at the heart of God's plan.

The first of Luke's additional "forgiven sinner" episodes seems to be an extensive revision of a story from Mark. Three days before his death, Mark's Jesus sits at table in the house of Simon the leper. A woman takes "an alabaster jar of very costly ointment" and pours it over Jesus' head. When a dispute arises over the wasted ointment, Jesus defends the woman (Mark 14:3-9).

---

9. Tannehill also highlights the relevant episodes (*Narrative Unity*, 1:103–27).

Luke uses the scene to set up a confrontation about forgiveness. He moves it toward the beginning of his story, changing most of the details (Luke 7:36-50). Luke's Jesus sits at table in the house of Simon the Pharisee. A woman with "an alabaster jar of ointment" pours it over Jesus' feet, washing them with her tears and drying them with her hair. "If this man were a prophet," thinks Simon, "he would have known who and what kind of woman this is who is touching him—that she is a sinner" (Luke 7:37-39).

In response, Jesus proves that he is indeed a prophet. He knows not only that the woman is a sinner but also what Simon is thinking. He tells Simon a prophetic parable about two debtors, one who owed much and one who owed little. Their creditor canceled both debts. "Which of them will love him more?" asks Jesus (Luke 7:42). Simon gives the obvious answer. This, says Jesus, explains Simon's lack of courtesy as well as the woman's extravagance. "Her sins, which were many, have been forgiven; hence she has shown great love" (Luke 7:47).

This raises an issue for Simon and his guests: can Jesus really forgive sins? Luke addresses the issue by borrowing language from Mark. As Mark's Jesus tells the paralytic, so Luke's Jesus tells the woman, "Your sins are forgiven" (Luke 7:48). This familiar statement leads to familiar reactions. The dinner guests ask, "Who is this, who even forgives sins?" (Luke 7:49). Luke's Jesus does not answer. Instead, he assures this woman as Mark's Jesus assures another woman: "Your faith has saved you; go in peace" (Luke 7:50; cf. Mark 5:34). The implication is clear: a prophet who reads minds might also have the power to forgive sins.

Luke's second "forgiven sinner" episode picks up where the scene in Levi's house left off. The situation is quite similar: "Now all the tax collectors and sinners [hamartōloi] were coming near to listen to him."[10] The Pharisees and scribes voice a similar concern: "This fellow welcomes sinners [prosdechetai hamartōloi] and eats with them" (Luke 15:1-2). In response, Jesus tells three parables that illustrate God's determination to save sinners. The first parable, borrowed from Q, concerns one of a hundred "sheep [probata]" that goes missing. For Matthew, the sheep that "has gone astray [planēthē]" is "one of these little ones," possibly a believer with few economic or spiritual resources (Matt. 18:6-14).[11] For Luke, however, the "lost [apolōlos] sheep" is "one sinner

---

10. The Greek New Testament text is taken from NA[28]. Significant variants are treated in the notes.

11. Some fifth-century manuscripts (e.g., Codex Bezae and Codex Washintonianus) include the following clause in Matt. 18:11: "For the Son of Man came to save the lost." If this clause belongs to Matthew's original text and could therefore be attributed to Q, it makes Luke's vocabulary less distinctive. It is unlikely, however, that it appeared in Luke's text of Q. Its absence from fourth-century manuscripts (Codex Sinaiticus and Codex Alexandrinus) indicates rather that it was added to Matt. 18:11,

[*hamartōlō*] who repents" (Luke 15:3-7). Luke follows with a second parable, unique to his Gospel, that tells the same kind of story: a woman "loses [*apolesē*]" a coin and must "search [*zētei*]" until she finds it (Luke 15:8-10). The series ends with the well-loved tale of the prodigal son, who "was lost [*apolōlōs*] and has been found" (Luke 15:11-32).

These three parables echo prophecies from Jeremiah and Ezekiel—prophecies that describe the people of Israel. "My people have become lost sheep [*probata apolōlata*]," complains Jeremiah; "their shepherds drove them out. They went astray [*apeplanēsan*] upon the mountains; they kept going from mountain to hill; they have forgotten their sheepfold. . . . They have sinned [*hēmarton*] against the Lord" (Jer. 50:6-7). Elsewhere, he affirms, "I myself will welcome [*eisdexomai*] the remnant of my people" (Jer. 23:3). Ezekiel confirms this promise: "I myself will shepherd my sheep [*probata*]. . . . I will seek the lost [*to apolōlos zētēsō*], and I will turn back the strayed [*planōmenon*]" (Ezek. 34:15-16). Luke seems to suggest that when Jesus welcomes sinners, these prophecies are being fulfilled. The Lord is seeking and finding his lost sheep.

The third episode introduces another tax collector—a chief tax collector, no less (Luke 19:1-10). After welcoming Jesus to his house, Zacchaeus announces his plan to follow John the Baptist's advice for repentant tax collectors (see Luke 3:12-13). He will give away half of his property and compensate everyone he has cheated. Jesus assures Zacchaeus, "Today salvation has come to this house, because he too is a son of Abraham" (Luke 19:9). Jesus closes the story with a nod to the parables of Luke 15:1-32 and the prophecy of Ezek. 34:15-16: "The Son of Man came to seek out [*zētēsai*] and to save the lost [*to apolōlos*]" (Luke 19:10). As a man looks for his lost sheep, as a woman searches for her lost coin, as a father welcomes his wayward son—so Jesus forgives all repentant Jews, even chief tax collectors.

Significantly, the Messiah's mission to save sinners continues at his execution. Luke borrows the relevant details from Mark, including the fact Jesus was crucified between two criminals (Luke 23:33//Mark 15:27). While Mark simply mentions that the criminals reviled Jesus, however, Luke details their conversation. One of them taunts the dying Jesus: "Are you not the Messiah? Save yourself and us!" The other, however, reminds the scoffer that they are getting their just deserts. "Jesus," he begs, "remember me when you come into your kingdom." Jesus reassures him with a prophecy: "Today you will be with me in Paradise" (Luke 23:39-43). Although he does not save himself or his

probably to harmonize with Luke 15:3-7; 19:10. See Bruce M. Metzger, *A Textual Commentary on the Greek New Testament* (Stuttgart: United Bible Societies, 1971), 44–45.

fellow Jews from the Romans, Jesus is indeed the Savior, from the moment of his birth right up to his last breath.[12]

After his resurrection, Luke's Jesus explains that his mission has only just begun. "Thus it is written," he says, "that the Messiah is to suffer and to rise from the dead on the third day, and that repentance and forgiveness of sins is to be proclaimed in his name" (Luke 24:46–47). Accordingly, when Jesus' followers preach the good news in the book of Acts, they issue a call: "Repent and be baptized . . . that your sins may be forgiven" (Acts 2:38).[13] Responding to this call is a matter of some urgency. As Peter explains to Cornelius, Jesus "is the one ordained by God as judge of the living and the dead" (Acts 10:42). Presumably, it is better to be forgiven now than to be judged when the Messiah returns at "the time of universal restoration" (Acts 3:21). Luke's apostles therefore extend the call to everyone, Jews and Gentiles alike. It meets with surprising responses and leads to catastrophic consequences. To explain, Luke must turn to the precedent set by Israel's prophets.

12. See also Richard I. Pervo, *Acts: A Commentary*, Hermeneia (Minneapolis: Fortress Press, 2008), 23.
13. The call is reiterated in Acts 3:19; 5:31; 10:43; 13:38–39; 17:30.

3

Trustworthy Prophets

Prophets set the precedent from the first two chapters of Luke's story. These chapters contain infancy narratives of Jesus and John the Baptist that do not appear in Mark or Q. They therefore bear the imprint of Luke's agenda. They introduce God's plan of salvation: a plan that includes everyone; a plan rejected by many in Israel; a plan that branches out from God's temple. They stress God's initiative in bringing Jesus and John into the world. They establish Jesus as the Messiah—the primary agent who will carry out God's plan—and John as his forerunner. They also legitimate God's plan by introducing Jesus and John as the prophets who set it in motion.

The prophetic precedent for the two infants is Samuel. Scholars frequently note the similarities between 1 Samuel 1–3 and Luke 1–2.[1] The parallels are hard to miss. Still, why does Luke choose Samuel and not some other prophet as a paradigm for the young John and Jesus? To which Samuel episodes does Luke allude? What agenda governs their selection?

---

1. Eric Burrows, "The Gospel of the Infancy: The Form of Luke Chapters 1 and 2," in *The Gospel of the Infancy and Other Biblical Essays*, The Bellarmine Series 6 (London: Burns, Oates & Washbourne, 1940), 2–27; G. W. H. Lampe, "The Holy Spirit in the Writings of St Luke," in *Studies in the Gospels*, ed. D. E. Nineham (Oxford: Blackwell, 1955), 166; Félix Gils, *Jésus prophète d'aprés les Évangiles synoptiques*, Orientalia et Biblica Lovaniensia 2 (Leuven: Publications Universitaires, 1957), 45; Raymond E. Brown, *The Birth of the Messiah: A Commentary on the Infancy Narratives in Matthew and Luke*, new ed., ABRL (New York: Doubleday, 1993), 267–69, 273, 357–58, 450–51, 469, 486, 494–95; David L. Tiede, *Prophecy and History in Luke-Acts* (Philadelphia: Fortress Press, 1980), 23; C. F. Evans, *Saint Luke*, TPINTC (London: SCM, 1990), 144–227; Robert C. Tannehill, *The Narrative Unity of Luke-Acts: A Literary Interpretation* (Philadelphia: Fortress Press, 1986), 1:18; Elisabeth Johnson, "Barrenness, Birth, and Biblical Allusions in Luke 1–2" (Ph.D. diss., Princeton Theological Seminary, 2000), 103–34. More recently, Kenneth D. Litwak has strenuously argued that Luke does not use 1 Sam. 1–2 as a basis for Jesus' infancy narrative ("A Coat of Many Colors: The Role of the Scriptures of Israel in Luke 2," in *Biblical Interpretation in Early Christian Gospels: The Gospel of Luke*, Library of New Testament Studies 376 [New York: T & T Clark, 2010], 128–30). I am not suggesting that he does. Instead, I am showing how Luke seems to use strategic allusions in order to make a point about Jesus' prophetic identity.

Luke's choice of Samuel is fairly easy to explain. His selection is limited to the two biblical prophets whose births and infancies receive any attention in Israel's Scriptures: Moses (Exod. 2:1-10) and Samuel (1 Sam. 1:1—4:1). Since Luke so freely compares the adult Jesus to the adult Moses, it is perhaps surprising that he does not extend the comparisons to their childhoods. The infant Moses, however, who was conceived in the usual way and rescued from Pharaoh only to be raised in Egypt's royal household, does not serve as a useful model for Luke. He does not much resemble the infants John or Jesus as Luke seeks to portray them.[2]

Samuel, however, offers many more possibilities. His story features God's favor to a woman, God's regard for the poor, and God's house.[3] Luke borrows several significant details. He starts with Hannah's childlessness, her prayer at God's house, and her nazirite vow on Samuel's behalf, applying them to the birth narrative of John the Baptist. Then, to illustrate Jesus' conception and infancy, he turns to Hannah's self-identification as God's lowly servant, her song of praise to God, who humbles the powerful and exalts the poor, and her son's childhood in God's shrine. Three times Luke informs his audience that, like Samuel, John and Jesus grew in body and spirit. In this way, he establishes John and Jesus as trustworthy prophets who will carry out God's plan—a plan that centers on the temple and reaches out to include the poor and lowly, men and women alike.[4]

---

2. In contrast, Matthew seems to find it quite useful to portray Jesus as an infant like Moses. Both are born under the rule of kings who kill baby boys (Matt. 2:16-18; cf. Exod. 1:15-22); the parents of both take steps to protect their sons (Matt. 2:13-15, 19-23; cf. Exod. 2:1-4); both come out of Egypt (Matt. 2:15; cf. Exod. 12:41). Matthew continues the parallels into Jesus' adult ministry: he spends forty days in the wilderness (Matt. 4:1-2; cf. Exod. 24:18; 34:28; Deut. 9:9); he leads twelve disciples (Matt. 10:1-4; cf. Exod. 24:3-4); he performs ten miracles (Matt. 8:1—9:34; cf. Exod. 7:14—12:32). Most importantly, he delivers five discourses (Matt. 5:1—7:27; 10:1-42; 13:1-52; 18:1-35; 24:3—25:46; cf. Genesis; Exodus; Leviticus; Numbers; Deuteronomy), seated on a mountain for the first and last (Matt. 5:1; 24:3; cf. Exod. 19:20; Deut. 34:1). For Matthew, apparently, Jesus is a teacher like Moses.

3. Samuel's story also features righteous Israelites, a motif that Luke finds useful in showing that Christians are not doing anything illegal. They are law-abiding Jews.

4. In contrast, Burrows argues that Luke uses Samuel parallels "to give his history the atmosphere of sacred scripture" ("Gospel of the Infancy," 1). Lampe suggests that Luke seeks to portray John as a preeminent prophet ("Holy Spirit in the Writings of St Luke," 166). Evans (*Saint Luke*), Tiede (*Prophecy and History*), and Tannehill (*Narrative Unity of Luke-Acts*) also focus on the parallels' general utility for portraying Jesus as a prophet. According to Elisabeth Johnson, they illustrate the fulfillment of God's promises to Abraham and David ("Barrenness, Birth, and Biblical Allusions," 264–65).

"The Prophet of the Most High"

Luke's account of God's plan begins with John's conception. The story, told in the vocabulary and style of the Septuagint, sets an important tone: God works in familiar ways. Luke needs to set this tone because God is about to do some unfamiliar things. God is about to send the Messiah who, along with his forerunner, will defy everyone's expectations. In order to stress that this is all God's doing, Luke tells how God brings Jesus and John on the scene as with other biblical heroes: heralded by angels and miraculously conceived.

Samuel is not the only biblical hero Luke has in mind. Others include Isaac, Jacob, Joseph, and Samson. Anyone familiar with their birth narratives would recognize the distinctive details and vocabulary in Luke 1. John's parents Zechariah and Elizabeth are "old [*presbytēs*]" and "getting on [*probebēkotes*] in years" (Luke 1:7, 18; cf. Gen. 18:11-12). Elizabeth is "barren [*steira*]," said to have "had no children" (Luke 1:7; cf. Gen. 11:30; 16:1; 25:21; 29:31; Judg. 13:2-3). When Zechariah is offering incense, "there appeared . . . an angel [*ōphthē angelos*] of the Lord" (Luke 1:11; cf. Gen. 18:1; Judg. 13:3). "Your prayer has been heard [*eisēkousthē hē deēsis sou*]," Gabriel says (Luke 1:13; cf. Gen. 25:21). Elizabeth will bear a son and Zechariah will "will name him [*kaleseis to onoma autou*] John" (Luke 1:13; cf. Gen. 17:19). John "must never drink wine or strong drink [*kai oinon kai sikera ou mē piē*]" (Luke 1:15; cf. Judg. 13:7, 14). When she conceives, Elizabeth says, "The Lord took away [my] disgrace [*aphelein oneidos mou*]" (Luke 1:25; cf. Gen. 30:23). When John and Jesus are born, their parents "circumcise [*peritemein*]" them "on the eighth day [*tē hēmera tē ogdoē*]" (Luke 1:59; 2:21; cf. Gen. 21:2-4). In each case, "the child [*to paidarion*]" then grows (*ēuxanen*) and becomes strong (Luke 1:80; 2:40; cf. Gen. 21:8; Judg. 13:24).[5]

God thus arranges for John's and Jesus' conceptions and births in very familiar ways. At the same time, however, their arrival marks the start of something new. According to Gabriel, John "will turn many of the people of Israel to the Lord their God. With the spirit and power of Elijah he will go before him, to turn the hearts of parents to their children [*epistrepsai kardias paterōn epi tekna*], and the disobedient to the wisdom of the righteous, to make ready a people prepared for the Lord" (Luke 1:16-17). God reaffirms this with a prophecy at John's birth. Zechariah, filled with the Holy Spirit, outlines the future mission of his infant son:

And you, child, will be called the prophet of the Most High;

---

5. Brown, *Birth of the Messiah*, 469.

> for you will go before the Lord to prepare his ways.
> (Luke 1:76)

John and Jesus may enter the scene as did Samson and the patriarchs, but they will act differently once they take the stage.

John's mission is new but not unforeseen. According to Mark and Q, it is described in Exod. 23:20; Mal. 3:1; and Isa. 40:3:

> See, I am sending my messenger ahead of you,
>   who will prepare your way;
> the voice of one crying out in the wilderness:
> "Prepare the way of the Lord,
>   make his paths straight." (Mark 1:2-3)
> See, I am sending my messenger ahead of you,
>   who will prepare your way before you. (Matt. 11:10)

Luke reproduces these traditions. He applies Mark's quotation of Isa. 40:3 to the beginning of John's adult ministry, identifying John as

> The voice of one crying out in the wilderness:
> "Prepare the way of the Lord,
>   make his paths straight." (Luke 3:3-4//Mark 1:2-3)

Later, in response to the query from the imprisoned John, Luke's Jesus confirms John's identity by citing Q's conflation of Exod. 23:20 and Mal. 3:1:

> This is the one about whom it is written,
> "See, I am sending my messenger ahead of you,
>   who will prepare your way before you." (Luke 7:27//Matt. 11:10)

Luke echoes these prophecies from Mark in Gabriel's and Zechariah's descriptions of John. He is the voice of Isa. 40:3 and the messenger of Exod. 23:20 and Mal. 3:1; the one who prepares the way of the Lord.

Gabriel's description also echoes a second prophecy found in Mal. 4:5-6: "And look, I am sending you Elijah the Tishbite before the great and remarkable day of the Lord comes. He will restore the heart of the father to the son [*apokatastēsei kardian patros pros huion*] and the heart of a man to his neighbor, so that I will not come and utterly strike the land." In Mark's Gospel, this prophecy refers to John. After witnessing the transfiguration, Peter, James, and John ask Jesus, "Why do the scribes say that Elijah must come first?" Mark's

Jesus replies, "Elijah is indeed coming first to restore [*apokatistanei*] all things" (Mark 9:11-12). He goes on to imply that Elijah has come in the person of John the Baptist. Luke simply shifts the allusion from the transfiguration scene to Gabriel's speech. John is none other than the Elijah figure foretold by Malachi; the prophet who restores Israel's heart before the day of the Lord.

Although Luke introduces John with an explicit comparison to Elijah, he does not otherwise stress the likeness. He does not emphasize John's physical resemblance to Elijah, nor does he depict John engaged in activities similar to Elijah's. This is interesting because Mark clearly does—and not just in the transfiguration episode. At the very beginning of Mark's Gospel, John appears in the wilderness "clothed with camel's hair, with a leather belt around his waist" (Mark 1:6). He is like Elijah, described in 2 Kgs. 1:8 as "a hairy man, with a leather belt around his waist." In addition, Mark's John relates to Herod and Herodias in the same way Elijah relates to Ahab and Jezebel. In both cases, the prophet confronts the king, and the king's wife conspires to have the prophet killed (Mark 6:14-29; cf. 1 Kgs. 19:1-3).

Luke omits all this material from Mark. He avoids reporting that John looked or acted like Elijah. He does not even explain that Herodias conspired to have John killed. More useful to Luke than the similarities between Elijah and John are the similarities between Elijah and Jesus.[6] Like Jesus, Elijah is a miracle-working prophet. He is "taken up," and his spirit is transferred to his disciple. John may carry out the mission of the future Elijah as foretold in Mal. 4:5-6, but Jesus looks more like the historical Elijah of 1 and 2 Kings.

The only biblical prophet whose story resembles John's is Samuel. Both have disgraced mothers whose vindication begins in God's house. For Luke, the disgraced mother is Elizabeth. She and Zechariah "[have] no children [*kai ouk ēn autois teknon*]" (Luke 1:7). In a society where women were expected to marry and have babies, infertility was not only a matter of personal anguish but also a matter of public disgrace. There was never a question that the cause of

---

6. See also Paul Hinnebusch, "Jesus, the New Elijah, in Saint Luke," *TBT* 31 (1967): 2176; Morna D. Hooker, *The Signs of a Prophet: The Prophetic Actions of Jesus* (Harrisburg, PA: Trinity Press International, 1997), 60–61. In contrast, P. Dabeck argues that Luke portrays John as a prophet like Elijah, the revealer of the Holy Spirit, just as Matthew portrays Jesus as a prophet like Moses, the revealer of the law ("Siehe, es erschienen Moses und Elias," *Bib* 23 [1942]: 180, 189). Walter Wink concludes that "Luke uses Elijah purely as a basis of comparison, in order to establish John as one of the great prophets" (*John the Baptist in the Gospel Tradition*, SNTSMS 7 [Cambridge: Cambridge University Press, 1968], 42–43). Paul S. Minear builds on this explanation: John's likeness to Elijah indicates his greatness and emphasizes his urgent call to repentance (*To Heal and to Reveal: The Prophetic Vocation According to Luke* [New York: Seabury, 1976], 95–96).

infertility might lie with the husband. If he had diligently planted his seeds, then the problem lay in his wife's womb. For some reason, God was cursing her with childlessness. She became a disappointment to her husband and his family as well as a failure in the eyes of her neighbors. As Luke explains, Elizabeth knows this all too well (Luke 1:25).

The turning point in Elizabeth's story takes place in the "sanctuary of the Lord [*ton naon tou kyriou*]" (Luke 1:9). Zechariah is offering incense "before God [*enanti tou theou*]" when the angel Gabriel appears to him (Luke 1:8-10). "Your prayer [*deēsis*] has been heard," announces the angel. "Your wife Elizabeth will bear you a son, and you will name him [*kaleseis to onoma autou*] John" (Luke 1:13-14). Soon afterward, Elizabeth conceives (*synelaben*). "This is what the Lord has done for me," she says, "when he looked favorably on me and took away the disgrace I have endured among my people" (Luke 1:25). God continues to keep his promise when, at the appropriate time, she "[gives] birth [*tekein*]" to "a son [*huion*]" (Luke 1:57).

All this is reminiscent of Samuel's mother Hannah. Although she has been married to Elkanah for several years, "Hannah [has] no children [*kai tē Anna ouk ēn paidion*]" (1 Sam. 1:2). Elkanah's other, more fertile wife harasses Hannah, causing her to weep and lose her appetite (1 Sam. 1:6-7). This leads Hannah to pray urgently for a son (1 Sam. 1:10-11). She pours out her soul "before the Lord [*enōpion kyriou*]" in the "sanctuary of the Lord [*naou kyriou*]" at Shiloh, where the ark of the covenant is enshrined (1 Sam. 1:9, 15). Her prayer is overheard by Eli the priest, who speaks a benediction over her: "Go in peace; the God of Israel grant the petition [*aitēma*] you have made of him" (1 Sam. 1:17). Soon afterward, Hannah conceives (*synelaben*). She "[bears a son [*eteken huion*]" and "[calls] his name [*ekalesen to onoma autou*]" Samuel (1 Sam. 1:20). The Lord has answered Hannah's prayer (1 Sam. 1:19-20, 27).

A barren woman; an encounter in God's sanctuary; an answered prayer; vindication from the Lord; the birth of a son—these parallels between Samuel's parents and John's parents help Luke illustrate the birth of a prophet as part of a divine plan that begins in the temple and shows favor to the disgraced. Luke goes on to draw two significant parallels between Samuel and John. For one, both are bound to the law for priests: "Drink no wine or strong drink [*oinon kai sikera ou piesthe*]" (Lev. 10:9). This law also pertains to anyone who takes a nazirite vow: "They shall separate themselves from wine and strong drink [*apo oinon kai sikera*]; they shall drink no vinegar made from wine or vinegar made from strong drink [*oxos ex oinou kai oxos ek sikera ou pietai*]" (Num. 6:3). Hannah makes the nazirite vow on behalf of the son she so desperately wants:

"He shall drink neither wine nor intoxicants [*oinon kai methysma ou pietai*]" (1 Sam. 1:11). In John's case, the angel simply informs Zechariah, "He must never drink wine or strong drink [*kai oinon kai sikera ou mē piē*]" (Luke 1:15). Lifelong abstinence from alcohol sets both prophets apart for God's service.

The other parallel between Samuel and John is that both boys grow and receive God's favor. Of Samuel, we learn that "the child [*to paidarion*] progressed and grew [*emegalyneto*] in favor both with the Lord and with the people" (1 Sam. 2:26). Similarly, Luke reports about John that "the child grew [*to de paidion ēuxanen*] and became strong in spirit" (Luke 1:80). Since this kind of detail adorns the infancy narrative of the prophet Samuel, Luke apparently considers it an appropriate conclusion to his story about John's conception and birth.

For John, as for Samuel, the conclusion points forward. God has brought the prophet into the world and set him apart. Since Samuel grew up to be "a trustworthy prophet of the Lord" (1 Sam. 3:20), we expect the same from John. The baby has already exhibited extraordinary prophetic sensibilities while still in his mother's womb: he recognized the gestating Messiah and leaped for joy (Luke 1:41, 44). Now that he is born, he will become an agent of God's plan.

John carries out his mission to proclaim "a baptism of repentance for the forgiveness of sins" in Luke 3:1-20. Luke bases this episode on stories from Mark and Q (Mark 1:2-11; Matt. 3:7-10, 12). Unlike his sources, however, Luke gives the adult John a prophet's introduction. "In the fifteenth year of the reign of Emperor Tiberius," he writes, "when Pontius Pilate was governor of Judea, and Herod was ruler of Galilee, and his brother Philip ruler of the region of Ituraea and Trachonitis, and Lysanias ruler of Abilene, during the high priesthood of Annas and Caiaphas, the word of God came to John son of Zechariah [*egeneto rhēma theou epi Iōannēn ton Zachariou huion*] in the wilderness" (Luke 3:1-2). This introduction, with its markers of time and place—and above all its statement that "the word of God came to" the prophet, whose father is also named—resembles the introductions of many biblical prophets.[7] Jeremiah's introduction offers the closest parallel: "The word of God that came to Jeremiah son of Hilkiah [*To rhēma theou, ho egeneto epi Ieremian ton tou Chelkiou*] of the priests, who lived in Anathoth in the land of Benjamin; a word of God that came to him in the days of Josiah son of Amon, king of Judah, in the thirteenth year of his reign. It came also in the days of Joachim son of Josiah, king of Judah, until the eleventh year of Zedekiah son of Josiah, king of Judah, until the captivity of Jerusalem in the fifth month" (Jer. 1:1-3).[8] By providing John with

---

7. See e.g. Ezek. 1:1-3; Hos. 1:1; Mic. 1:1; Zeph. 1:1; Hag. 1:1; Zech. 1:1.

a similar introduction, Luke has gone out of his way to remind his readers that the one who had a prophet's birth has now embarked on a prophet's career.[9]

That career features prophetic oracles, some borrowed from Luke's sources. John warns the crowds that if their repentance is not genuine, they will suffer God's wrath (Luke 3:7-9, 17//Matt. 3:7-10, 12). He also foretells the coming of one who "will baptize . . . with the Holy Spirit and fire" (Luke 3:16//Mark 1:8). In these speeches, John fulfills God's word proclaimed by Gabriel and Zechariah. He goes before the Messiah "with the spirit and power of Elijah," turning "the disobedient to the wisdom of the righteous, to make ready a people prepared for the Lord" and giving "knowledge of salvation to his people by the forgiveness of their sins" (Luke 1:17, 77).

Luke not only reiterates Mark's and Q's references to John's prophetic oracles but also preserves their intimations of John's prophetic identity. Jesus himself confirms that John is a prophet—and "more than a prophet" (Luke 7:26//Matt. 11:9). The people are also convinced of it (Luke 20:6//Matt. 21:26). They place John in the same league as Elijah and other ancient prophets (Luke 9:7-8, 19//Mark 6:14-15; 8:28).

Most importantly, Luke portrays John as a prophet who ministers to everyone. He introduces the adult John with a quotation from Isaiah 40—a quotation that he borrows from Mark 1:3 and extends for two extra verses:

The voice of one crying out in the wilderness:
   "Prepare the way of the Lord,
      make his paths straight.
   Every valley shall be filled,
      and every mountain and hill shall be made low,
   and the crooked shall be made straight,
      and the rough ways made smooth;
   and all flesh shall see the salvation of God." (Luke 3:4-6; cf. Isa. 40:3-5)

By extending the quotation, Luke neatly clarifies that the salvation proclaimed by John is not for Jews only. It is available to "all flesh."

To illustrate, Luke adds to John's subsequent warnings as copied from Q. "Bear fruits worthy of repentance," John admonishes the crowds (Luke 3:8//Matt. 3:8). "What then should we do?" they ask (Luke 3:10). This is John's cue to describe various acts of repentance. For average people, these include

---

8. Henry J. Cadbury, *The Making of Luke-Acts*, 3rd ed. (Peabody, MA: Hendrickson, 1999), 207–8.

9. Lampe, "Holy Spirit in the Writings of St Luke," 166; Tannehill, *Narrative Unity of Luke-Acts*, 1:47–48.

sharing food and clothing with those who have none. Tax collectors should gather their quota and no more; soldiers should not abuse their authority (Luke 3:11-14). The presence of tax collectors and soldiers, however, is a cause for some concern. Tax collectors, who diverted Israel's wealth to its Roman overlords, were among the most notorious Jewish sinners. Soldiers presumably were Roman soldiers—the very Gentile occupiers that the Messiah was meant to have dashed in pieces like a potter's vessel. What are they doing among the crowds baptized by John? According to Luke, such people are included in God's plan of salvation, even from its very beginning in John's ministry.

Sadly, John's proclamation of universal salvation does not make him universally popular. Since he pursues a prophet's career, he suffers a prophet's fate: rejection by influential Jews. Luke emphasizes that, unlike tax collectors, Pharisees and lawyers refuse John's baptism (Luke 7:29-30). Next, John treads on the toes of Herod Antipas, calling him to account for his incestuous marriage and other evil deeds. Herod imprisons him and eventually has him beheaded (Luke 3:19-20; 9:9; cf. Mark 6:17, 27). John has turned many in Israel to the Lord—but not all. Some have rejected John's baptism of repentance for the forgiveness of their sins.

"THE MESSIAH, THE LORD"

Luke is careful to distinguish between the prophetic mission of John and that of Jesus. John goes before the Lord (Luke 1:17), but—according to the angel who heralds his birth—Jesus is "the Messiah, the Lord" (Luke 2:11). John is "the prophet of the Most High" (Luke 1:76), but—in the words of Gabriel—Jesus is "the Son of the Most High" who will inherit "the throne of his ancestor David" (Luke 1:32-33). John himself acknowledges that, whereas he baptizes with water, Jesus baptizes with the Holy Spirit (Luke 3:16//Mark 1:8).[10] There is even a clear distinction in the manner of their conceptions. John, like Samuel, is born to a previously infertile couple. Jesus, however, is born to a "virgin [*parthenos*]" (Luke 1:27, 34). As Gabriel explains to Mary, "And now [*idou*], you will conceive in your womb [*syllēmphē en gastri*] and bear a son [*kai texē huion*]" (Luke 1:31). Presumably, this fulfills Isa. 7:14: "Look [*idou*], the virgin [*parthenos*] will conceive in the womb [*en gastri hexei*] and she will bear a son [*kai texetai huion*]." John's father is Zechariah, but Jesus' father is God.

These essential differences do not stop Luke from using Samuel as a model for Jesus' conception and birth as he does for John's. For Luke, Jesus—like Samuel and John—is a trustworthy prophet.[11] He, too, will get his start in God's

---

10. Cf. Acts 19:1-7.

sanctuary. From there, he will become an even more important agent of God's plan to extend salvation to all flesh.

Luke begins with parallels between Jesus' and Samuel's parents. First, he shows that Mary, like Hannah, views herself as a lowly servant whom God has favored. Gabriel begins his annunciation to Mary by explaining, "You have found favor [*heures gar charin*] with God" (Luke 1:30). In response to Gabriel's startling message, Mary answers, "Here am I, the servant [*doulē*] of the Lord" (Luke 1:38). She later acknowledges that God "has looked with favor on the lowliness of his servant [*epeblepsen epi tēn tapeinōsin tēs doulēs autou*]" (Luke 1:48). This statement is highly reminiscent of Hannah's prayer: "Look on the humiliation of your servant [*epiblepōn epiblepsēs epi tēn tapeinōsin tēs doulēs sou*] and give . . . your servant [*tē doulē sou*] male offspring" (1 Sam 1:11). It also recalls her response to the intercession of God's priest Eli: "Let your servant find favor [*heuren hē doulē sou charin*] in your sight" (1 Sam 1:18). God draws these lowly women into the center of divine activity.

This theme inspires Mary's song in Luke 1:46-55, an echo of Hannah's prayer in 1 Sam. 2:1-10.[12] Each begins with a personal declaration of praise:

My soul magnifies the Lord [*ton kyrion*],
    and my spirit rejoices in God my Savior [*epi tō theō tō sōtēri mou*]. (Luke 1:46)

My heart is made strong in the Lord [*en kyriō*];
    my horn is exalted in my God [*en theō mou*]. (1 Sam. 2:1)

Mary and Hannah praise God with heart and soul, body and spirit, because God has reversed their social circumstances. Hannah, a despised, childless woman, is now the proud mother of a son. "She who was barren has borne seven children,"

---

11. Several scholars note the parallels between the infants Jesus and John. Cadbury attributes them to narrative assimilation (*Making of Luke-Acts*, 233). Charles H. Talbert focuses on Luke's view of salvation history in which the ministry of Jesus is continuous with the ministry of his forerunner (*Literary Patterns, Theological Themes and the Genre of Luke-Acts* [Missoula, MT: Scholars Press, 1974], 44, 106). I stress the prophetic nature of both ministries. See also Eric Franklin, *Christ the Lord: A Study in the Purpose and Theology of Luke-Acts* (Philadelphia: Westminster, 1975), 200n41.

12. Lines from 1 Samuel 2:2, 5, and 8 are reiterated in Ps. 113:5, 7-8. Mary's song borrows not only from Hannah's song but also from Leah's benedictions (Gen. 29:32; 30:13), Isaiah's affirmations of God's faithfulness to Israel (Isa. 40:10; 41:8-10; 51:9), and various psalms of praise (e.g., Pss. 34:3-4; 35:9; 103:17; 107:9).

she boasts (1 Sam 2:5). Likewise, Mary leaves the obscurity of Nazareth to mother the Messiah. Her response:

> Surely, from now on all generations will call me blessed;
>> for the Mighty One has done great things for me,
>>> and holy is his name. (Luke 1:48-49)

Both women acknowledge that they are not the only ones whose lives are turned upside down. God is in the business of reversal. God brings down the rich and the powerful. God lifts up the hungry and the poor.

> He has looked with favor on the lowliness [*tapeinōsin*] of his servant.
> . . .
> He has brought down the powerful [*dynastas*] from their thrones [*thronōn*],
>> and lifted up the lowly [*hypsōsen tapeinous*];
> he has filled the hungry [*peinōntas*] with good things,
>> and sent the rich [*ploutountas*] away empty. (Luke 1:48, 52-53)

> Those who were full of bread have too little,
>> and those who are hungry [*hoi peinōntes*] forsake the land.
> . . .
> The Lord makes poor and makes rich [*ploutizei*];
>> he brings low [*tapeinoi*], he also lifts up [*anypsoi*].
> He lifts up the poor from the earth;
>> he raises the beggar from the dunghill,
> to make them sit with the princes [*dynastōn*] of the people
>> and inherit a throne [*thronon*] of glory. (1 Sam. 2:5, 7-8)

Mary, the mother of Jesus, reaffirms what Hannah, the mother of Samuel, has already proclaimed: that God exalts the poor, the hungry, the lowly, the barren wife of Elkanah, the virgin from Nazareth.

Once Luke has illustrated the precedent that Hannah sets for Mary, he goes on to portray the young Jesus as a prophet like Samuel. Like Samuel, Jesus is formed by time spent in the Lord's sanctuary. Luke demonstrates this on two separate occasions. He first informs his audience that, forty days after his birth, Jesus' parents "brought him to Jerusalem to present him to the Lord [*anēgagon auton eis Hierosolyma parastēsai tō kyriō*]" (Luke 2:22). This is to assure them that Mary and Joseph adhere to God's laws concerning the consecration of firstborn children and the purification of a woman following the birth of a son.[13] As prescribed in Lev. 12:8, they offer two birds—either turtledoves or pigeons—for Mary's purification.

None of the laws for consecrating a firstborn son, however, requires that the child be brought to the sanctuary. Luke's Mary and Joseph bring Jesus to the temple not in obedience to a commandment but in imitation of Hannah. She, too, brings her son Samuel to God's house. She has vowed not to make the annual pilgrimage with her husband "until the child goes up, when I wean him; then he will appear in the presence of the Lord and stay there forever" (1 Sam. 1:22). Accordingly, when Samuel is weaned, she "[goes] up with him to Shiloh [*anabē met' autou eis Sēlōm*]," bringing a bull calf along with offerings of bread, flour, and wine (1 Sam. 1:24). There she and her husband Elkanah "[bring] him before the Lord [*prosēgagon enōpion kyriou*]" (1 Sam. 1:25).[14]

Jesus resembles Samuel not only in being brought to the temple and presented to the Lord in his infancy but also in being recognized as a prodigy there in his youth.[15] In Samuel's case, he is "sleeping in the shrine [*en tō naō*] . . . where the ark of God was" when God calls him by name: "Samuel, Samuel!" (1 Sam. 3:3-4). Eli the priest cannot hear God's voice; he can only advise Samuel how to respond. "Speak, Lord, for your servant is listening," says the boy (1 Sam. 3:9-10). There in the sanctuary at Shiloh God gives Samuel his first prophetic word: a judgment oracle against his mentor Eli.

Jesus does not live at the shrine as Samuel does, but his parents (like Samuel's parents) make an annual pilgrimage. Naturally, Jesus goes with them. One Passover, the twelve-year-old Jesus remains "in the temple [*en tō hierō*]" after the festival, amazing the teachers while his exasperated parents search for him everywhere (Luke 2:41-46). He greets them with an unusual question: "Did you not know that I must be in my Father's house?" (Luke 2:49). The young Jesus astounds his elders in the sanctuary in Jerusalem, displaying preternatural understanding both of God's word and of his own identity as God's son. The scene is a preview of things to come. When he next appears in

---

13. For the laws concerning the firstborn, see Exod. 13:2; 22:29-30; 34:19-20; Num. 18:15-16. The rules governing purification after childbirth can be found in Lev. 12:1-8.

14. The verb *prosagein* is used three times in 1 Sam. 1:25.

15. Donald Juel, *Luke-Acts: The Promise of History* (Atlanta: John Knox, 1983), 25.

the temple, Jesus will confound the teachers and, like Samuel, issue a judgment oracle against them (Luke 20:9-19).

Luke rounds off his portrayal of Jesus as a prophet like Samuel with a technique he has also used in his portrayal of John the Baptist: providing notices of the child's physical and spiritual growth. Samuel's infancy narrative contains two such notices:

> The boy [*to paidarion*] Samuel grew up [*emegalynthē*] before the Lord. (1 Sam. 2:21)

> Now the child [*to paidarion*] progressed and grew [*emegalyneto*] in favor both with the Lord and with the people [*kai meta anthrōpōn*]. (1 Sam. 2:26)

We have already identified one similar statement about John:

> The child [*to de paidion ēuxanen*] grew and became strong in spirit. (Luke 1:80)

Luke adds two more notices about Jesus:

> The child grew [*to de paidion ēuxanen*] and became strong,
> filled with wisdom; and the favor of God was upon him. (Luke 2:40)
> Jesus increased in wisdom and years, and in divine and human [*kai anthrōpois*] favor. (Luke 2:52)

Verbal parallels are scant, but the structure and significance of these sentences make the allusions obvious.[16] They establish Jesus as "a trustworthy prophet of the Lord" (1 Sam. 3:20); a prophet whose mother is an insignificant virgin from Nazareth; a prophet whose career begins in the Jerusalem temple. These may seem like unusual beginnings for Israel's Messiah, but Luke's audience should not be concerned. They are typical beginnings for a prophet—and Samuel sets the precedent.

---

16. Lampe, "Holy Spirit in the Writings of St Luke," 175.

4

"A Light for the Gentiles"

The prophet Samuel does not provide an appropriate model for the adult Messiah as Luke portrays him. Samuel's wars with the Philistines, confrontations with Saul, and anointing of Jesus' royal progenitor David serve no useful purpose in illuminating Jesus' ministry and death. After Luke recounts Jesus' conception, birth, and childhood, he must rely on other prophets to set the precedent for Gentile inclusion, Jewish rejection, and the fall of Jerusalem. Elijah is a perfect candidate. He raises a dead child, as does the Jesus Luke knows from Mark's Gospel. More importantly, Elijah can help with Luke's agenda. God sends him to a Gentile; he transfers his spirit to his disciple. Luke can therefore use Elijah to legitimate the unexpected extension of God's salvation to all people—first through the Messiah, then through his followers.[1]

1. On the necessity for Luke to address this issue, see David L. Tiede, *Prophecy and History in Luke-Acts* (Philadelphia: Fortress Press, 1980), 120. Many scholars recognize some or all of the parallels discussed in this chapter. According to P. Dabeck, Adrian Hastings, and J. Severino Croatto, they illustrate various characteristics of Jesus such as his compassion and ability to heal (see Dabeck, "Siehe, es erschienen Moses und Elias," *Bib* 23 [1942]: 184–88; Hastings, *A Prophet and Witness in Jerusalem: A Study of the Teaching of Saint Luke* [London: Longmans, Green, & Co., 1958], 74–75; Croatto, "Jesus, Prophet Like Elijah, and Prophet-Teacher Like Moses in Luke-Acts," *JBL* 124, no. 3 [2005]: 461). Jean-Daniel Dubois, Paul S. Minear, and Ulrich Busse argue that the parallels liken Jesus to a prophet (see Dubois, "La Figure d'Elie dans la Perspective Lucanienne," *RHPR* 53 [1973]: 176; Minear, *To Heal and to Reveal: The Prophetic Vocation According to Luke* [New York: Seabury, 1976], 95–97; Busse, *Die Wunder des Propheten Jesus: Die Rezeption, Komposition und Interpretation der Wundertradition im Evangelium des Lukas*, FB 24 [Stuttgart: Katholisches Bibelwerk, 1977], 378). Paul Hinnebusch and Luke Timothy Johnson get more specific: the parallels liken Jesus to Elijah (Hinnebusch, "Jesus, the New Elijah, in Saint Luke," *TBT* 31 [1967]: 2176) or Moses (Johnson, *The Gospel of Luke*, SP 3 [Collegeville, MN: Liturgical, 1991], 119–20, 162–64). Craig A. Evans, D. A. S. Ravens, and Robert F. O'Toole take a different tack: the parallels illustrate themes like election, Jewish rejection, and salvation history (Evans, "Luke's Use of the Elijah/Elisha Narratives and the Ethics of Election," *JBL* 106 [1987]: 82, Ravens, "Luke 9.7-62 and the Prophetic Role of Jesus," *NTS* 36 [1990]: 128; O'Toole, *Luke's Presentation of Jesus: A Christology*, SubBi 25 [Rome: Editrice Pontifico Istituto Biblico, 2004], 52). My view that they legitimate Gentile outreach is shared by G. W. H. Lampe, Gerhard Voss, and Joel B. Green (Lampe, "The Holy Spirit in the Writings of St

"For All the People"

Luke consistently emphasizes that God offers salvation to everyone. As the angel tells the shepherds, the birth of the Messiah is "good news of great joy for all the people" (Luke 2:10). Simeon affirms this. Filled with the Holy Spirit, he takes the infant Jesus into his arms and prays:

> Master, now you are dismissing your servant in peace
> > according to your word;
> for my eyes have seen your salvation,
> > which you have prepared in the presence of all peoples;
> a light for revelation to the Gentiles [*phōs ethnōn*]
> > and for glory to your people Israel. (Luke 2:29-32)

Simeon's prophecy echoes Isa. 49:6:

> See, I have set you to be a covenant for the nation,
> > a light for the Gentiles [*phōs ethnōn*],
> so that you may bring salvation to the ends of the earth [*heōs eschatou tēs gēs*].

Luke reiterates this prophecy twice in the book of Acts. First, the risen Jesus tells his disciples, "You will be my witnesses . . . to the ends of the earth [*heōs eschatou tēs gēs*]" (Acts 1:8). Later, Paul quotes Isa. 49:6 as his personal mission statement:

> I have set you to be a light for the Gentiles,
> > so that you may bring salvation to the ends of the earth. (Acts 13:47)

By the time Barnabas brings Paul to Antioch (Acts 11:26), salvation for Gentiles has come to the fore. Meanwhile, Luke has introduced several more prophecies about salvation for everyone. When John the Baptist appears in the

Luke," in *Studies in the Gospels*, ed. D. E. Nineham [Oxford: Blackwell, 1955], 173; Voss, *Die Christologie der lukanischen Schriften in Grundzügen*, StudNeot 2 [Paris: Desclée de Brouwer, 1965], 158; Green, *The Gospel of Luke*, NICNT [Grand Rapids: Eerdmans, 1997], 381].

wilderness, Luke follows Mark in quoting Isa. 40:3—and keeps quoting through Isa. 40:5: "And all flesh shall see the salvation of God" (Luke 3:4-6; cf. Mark 1:3). A similar citation opens the book of Acts. When devout Jews question why the apostles are speaking in tongues, Peter explains that Joel 2:28-32 is being fulfilled:

> In the last days it will be, God declares,
> that I will pour out my Spirit upon all flesh,
>> and your sons and daughters shall prophesy,
> and your young men shall see visions,
>> and your old men shall dream dreams.
> Even upon my slaves, both men and women,
>> in those days I will pour out my Spirit. . . .
> Then everyone who calls on the name of the Lord shall be
> saved. (Acts 2:17-21)

Note how Joel uses synecdoche to explicate the term "everyone." Sons and daughters, young and old, men and women: God will pour out the Spirit on "all flesh."

Luke seems to take this prophecy literally, showing how Jesus saves male and female, children and adults. Luke's Jesus also includes various classes of disadvantaged people. This, too, is foretold in Scripture. In a scene borrowed from Q, John the Baptist asks, "Are you the one who is to come, or are we to wait for another?" Jesus responds by stating the nature of his mission: "The blind receive their sight, the lame walk, the lepers are cleansed, the deaf hear, the dead are raised, the poor have good news brought to them" (Luke 7:19, 22//Matt. 11:3, 5). This statement alludes to prophecies from Isaiah:

> Then the eyes of the blind shall be opened,
>> and the ears of the deaf will hear;
> then the lame shall leap like a deer,
>> and the language of those who stammer will be clear. (Isa.
> 35:5-6)

> The dead will arise, and those in the tombs will be lifted up. (Isa.
> 26:19)

> The spirit of the Lord is upon me,
>> because he has anointed me;
>> he has sent me to bring good news to the poor;
>>> to heal the brokenhearted;
>> to proclaim release to the captives
>>> and recovery of sight to the blind;
>> to announce the year of the Lord's favor. (Isa. 61:1-2)

John—as well as Luke's audience—can rest assured. Jesus may not look like the victorious king of Psalm 2 or the righteous judge of Isaiah 11, but he does seem to fulfill Isaiah's prophecies about rescue for the needy.

Luke finds Isa. 61:1-2 so useful that he adds it to one of Mark's stories: the account of Jesus' rejection at Nazareth. In Mark's Gospel, Jesus comes to Nazareth after traveling around Galilee (Mark 6:1-6). Luke, however, moves the incident closer to the beginning of his narrative, making it the first of Jesus' public acts (Luke 4:16-30). He uses Jesus' rejection at Nazareth to set the stage for the rest of his two-volume work.[2]

In order to shape Mark's story for his purposes, Luke significantly expands it.[3] Mark's account is quite simple. He reports that Jesus taught in his hometown synagogue, astonishing and then offending his friends and neighbors. They cannot believe the power and wisdom of the carpenter's son. Jesus' response: "Prophets are not without honor, except in their hometown, and among their own kin, and in their own house" (Mark 6:4).

This saying has an obvious utility for Luke. What better way to portray a rejected prophet than in a story about rejection in his own hometown—a story with a line about dishonored prophets? And what better way to explain why he was rejected than to fill in a few details? Luke therefore adds Jesus' sermon text and sermon. He then explains exactly what Jesus said to offend the congregation.

---

2. Henry J. Cadbury, *The Making of Luke-Acts*, 3rd ed. (Peabody, MA: Hendrickson, 1999), 189; Johnson, *Gospel of Luke*, 82.

3. Voss, *Die Christologie der lukanischen*, 156.

The sermon text is Isa. 61:1-2, conflated with a line from Isa. 58:6:

> The Spirit of the Lord is upon me,
>> because he has anointed me to bring good news to the
> poor.
> He has sent me to proclaim release to the captives
>> and recovery of sight to the blind,
>>> to let the oppressed go free,
> to proclaim the year of the Lord's favor. (Luke 4:18-19)

This prophecy states everything Luke wants to convey about Jesus' mission. The Holy Spirit rests on Jesus. God has "anointed [*echrisen*]" Jesus, making him the Messiah, the Christ. What is more, the anointing has a purpose: a mission to those in need. Isaiah has said it all. Luke's Jesus needs only to add, "Today this scripture has been fulfilled in your hearing" (Luke 4:21).

At first, the congregation is impressed. Joseph's son has become such an eloquent teacher! Jesus is not finished, however. First, he remarks that "no prophet is accepted in the prophet's hometown" (Luke 4:24//Mark 6:4). Then he offers an illustration: two prophets who ministered not to needy Israelites but to needy Gentiles. God sent the prophet Elijah to a Sidonian widow (Luke 4:25-26; cf. 1 Kgs. 17:9). The prophet Elisha cleansed a Syrian leper (Luke 4:27; cf. 2 Kgs. 5:1-14). Surely it was not lost on Luke that Elijah and Elisha were not well received in Israel.[4] Elijah and Elisha therefore establish an important precedent: when Israel is disinclined to listen to God's prophets, God sends them to Gentiles. This in turn leads to an important corollary: it would not be out of character for God to send his Anointed One—a Spirit-filled prophet, rejected in his own hometown—to Gentiles as well.

When Jesus leaves Nazareth, we might therefore expect that he would forego ministry to Jews and direct his attention to the local Gentile population. If so, we would be disappointed, because Luke's Jesus goes on to heal a Jewish leper and resuscitate the son of a Jewish widow (Luke 5:12-14; 7:11-17). Luke avoids depicting any direct contact between Jesus and Gentiles. He even alters his sources to this effect. For example, he omits a large section of Mark: everything between the feeding of the five thousand and the Pharisees' demand

---

4. 1 Kgs. 18:17; 19:1-2; 21:20; 2 Kgs. 3:13; 6:30-31.

for a sign (Mark 6:45—8:10). He does this partly because it includes stories about Jesus' Gentile ministry. Mark's Jesus redefines purity to exclude the kind of ritual purity most associated with Gentiles (Mark 7:14-23).[5] Mark's Jesus converses with a Syrophoenician woman and feeds a crowd of four thousand—Gentiles, judging by the setting and the kind of baskets they carry (Mark 7:24-30; 8:1-10).[6] Luke leaves these stories out.

Luke also changes Q's story about the centurion's slave. While Q's centurion approaches Jesus directly, Luke's centurion sends a delegation of Jewish elders (Matt. 8:5; Luke 7:3). Q's centurion says, "I am not worthy" (Matt. 8:8). So does Luke's centurion, but the Jewish elders have already contradicted him: "He is worthy of having you do this for him, for he loves our people, and it is he who built our synagogue for us" (Luke 7:4-6).[7] Luke stresses that this Roman army officer is the kind of Gentile who deserves attention from God's Messiah.[8] Still, Luke's Jesus keeps his distance. He heals the slave yet never meets the centurion face to face. He associates only with Israelites.

Some Israelites are sinners, so Jesus forgives them.[9] He chastises the rich and advocates for the poor.[10] He restores the demon possessed; he heals the diseased and disabled; he raises the dead.[11] Luke is careful to include the blind, the lame,

---

5. Luke does not redefine ritual purity until Acts 10:9-29.

6. Mark's Jesus feeds the four thousand in the region of the Decapolis, known for its large Gentile population. The people carry *spyridas*, baskets typically used by Gentiles. Jews preferred the smaller *kophinous*, mentioned in the previous feeding scene (Mark 6:43).

7. Since Luke's version complicates the story, it is likely that Matthew more accurately copies the original Q passage.

8. Some scholars suggest parallels between this story and the story of Elisha and Naaman (see, e.g., Thomas L. Brodie, "Towards Unraveling the Rhetorical Imitation of Sources in Acts: 2 Kings 5 as One Component of Acts 8,9-40," *Bib* 67 [1986]: 41–67; D. A. S. Ravens, "The Setting of Luke's Account of the Anointing: Luke 7.2—8.3," *NTS* 34 [1988]: 287). Johnson suggests that Luke alters Q's version in order to evoke 2 Kgs. 5:1-19 (*The Literary Function of Possessions in Luke-Acts*, SBLDS 39 [Missoula, MT: Scholars, 1977], 98; *Gospel of Luke*, 120). There is no verbal correspondence between the two episodes, however. It seems better to conclude that Luke alters Q's story for other reasons: to prevent Jesus from coming into contact with a Gentile; to portray the Gentile as a worthy object of Jesus' attention; to lay the groundwork for a second centurion story in Acts 10.

9. Luke 5:17-26//Mark 2:1-12; Luke 5:27-32//Mark 2:13-17; Luke 7:36-50//Mark 14:3-9; Luke 15:1-32; 19:1-10; 23:39-43//Mark 15:32.

10. Luke 6:20-26//Matt 5:3-6; Luke 12:13-21; 14:7-14; 16:19-31; 18:18-25//Mark 10:17-25. In Luke 14:21, a servant invites "the poor, the crippled, the blind, and the lame" to his master's banquet. He seems to have added this detail to a parable known also to Matthew (Matt. 22:1-10).

11. For exorcisms, see Luke 4:31-37, 41//Mark 1:21-28, 34; Luke 8:26-39//Mark 5:1-20; healings, Luke 4:38-40//Mark 1:30-33; Luke 5:12-16//Mark 1:40-45; Luke 5:17-26//Mark 2:1-12; Luke 6:6-11//Mark 3:1-6; Luke 7:1-10//Matt. 8:5-13; Luke 8:43-48//Mark 5:25-34; Luke 9:37-43//Mark

the lepers, the deaf, and the dead among these sufferers.[12] To Mark's accounts of sinful men, Luke adds a sinful woman; to the disabled man in a synagogue, a disabled woman in a synagogue; to the dead girl and her father, a dead man and his mother; to the male disciples, some female disciples.[13] Clearly, Luke's Jesus fulfills the prophecies of Isaiah and Joel.[14] Moreover, by raising dead children, he acts like Elijah.

"In the Time of Elijah"

Luke first hints at the Elijah resemblance early in his narrative when, in an episode borrowed from Mark, God leads Jesus "in the wilderness [*en tē erēmō*]," where he spends "forty days [*hēmeras tesserakonta*]" without food (Luke 4:2//Mark 1:13; cf. 1 Kgs. 19:1, 8).[15] Shortly afterward, Luke introduces the Elijah paradigm in Jesus' sermon at Nazareth: "Elijah was sent . . . to a widow at Zarephath in Sidon" (Luke 4:26). This sets up the story of the dead man and his mother (Luke 7:11-17). The mother is a widow, and the man is her only son. Jesus faces a situation similiar to that of Elijah who, after having saved the Sidonian widow and her only son from starvation, loses the boy to a severe illness (1 Kgs. 17:1-24).[16]

In many ways, Luke's account proceeds differently from the Elijah story. Luke's Jesus does not take the corpse to an upper room, nor does he lie

9:14-29; Luke 13:10-17; 14:1-6; 17:11-19; 18:35-42//Mark 10:46-52; Luke 22:51; resuscitations, Luke 7:11-17; 8:49-56//Mark 5:35-43.

12. Luke 5:12-26//Mark 1:40—2:12; Luke 7:11-17; 8:49-56//Mark 5:35-43; Luke 14:1-6; 17:11-19; Luke 18:35-42//Mark 10:46-52.

13. For sinful men and women, see Luke 5:17-26//Mark 2:1-12; Luke 5:27-32//Mark 2:13-17; Luke 7:36-50//Mark 14:3-9; Luke 19:1-10; 23:39-43//Mark 15:32; for the disabled man and woman, Luke 6:6-11//Mark 3:1-6; Luke 13:10-17; for the dead girl and the dead man, Luke 7:11-17; 8:49-56//Mark 5:35-43; for male and female disciples, Luke 6:12-16//Mark 3:13-19; Luke 8:1-3; Acts 1:13-14; 5:14; 17:4, 12. Other male-female pairs in Luke-Acts include Simeon and Anna (Luke 2:25-38), Aeneas and Dorcas (Acts 9:32-43), Dionysius and Damaris (Acts 17:33), Priscilla and Aquila (Acts 18:1-3, 18, 26), and Agabus plus the four daughters of Philip (Acts 21:9-11).

14. Cadbury, one of the first to observe Luke's male and female pairs, attributes them to Luke's style (*Making of Luke-Acts*, 234–35). I would go a step further and suggest that Luke shapes his narrative into a fulfillment of Isa. 40:5 interpreted in light of Joel 2:28-29. Robert C. Tannehill and Beverly R. Gaventa also point out the connection between Luke's emphasis on male and female and his prominent reference to the Joel passage (Tannehill, *The Narrative Unity of Luke-Acts: A Literary Interpretation* [Philadelphia: Fortress Press, 1986], 1:134; Gaventa, *The Acts of the Apostles*, ANTC [Nashville: Abingdon, 2003], 43).

15. See also Hastings, *Prophet and Witness*, 68.

16. Ibid., 71; Evans, "Luke's Use of the Elijah/Elisha Narratives," 79n22; François Bovon, *Luke 1: A Commentary on the Gospel of Luke 1:1—9:50*, Hermeneia (Minneapolis: Fortress Press, 2002), 268.

on it three times praying for life to be restored. Instead, he sticks to child-resuscitation techniques already reported in Mark's story of Jairus's daughter (Mark 5:35-43). Mark's Jesus encounters the corpse surrounded by weeping mourners. He assures the distraught parent before addressing the child: "Little girl, get up [*soi legō, egeire*]!" (Mark 5:36-41). The child then gets up and performs some proof of reanimation, astounding the witnesses (Mark 5:42-43). Luke's story recapitulates all these details, even down to the command, "I say to you, rise [*soi legō, egerthēti*]!" (Luke 7:12-16).[17] At the end of the story, however, Luke's Jesus makes a gesture not found in Mark: "Jesus gave him to his mother [*kai edōken auton tē mētri autou*]" (Luke 7:15). Luke has lifted the clause from 1 Kgs. 17:23. The people of Nain respond accordingly: "A great prophet has risen among us" (Luke 7:16).[18]

Their declaration is followed in quick succession by five episodes that underscore the similarity between Jesus and Elijah. First, Jesus raises Jairus's daughter. Luke reiterates details from Mark's version, already echoed in the story of the widow's son: mourners weep and wail; Jesus reassures the girl's parents; he commands the dead child to "get up [*egeire*]"; the girl gets up and eats; the parents are astounded (Luke 8:49-56//Mark 5:35-43). These reverberations alert Luke's audience to the fact that Jesus, a prophet like Elijah, is raising another dead child. As if this were not enough, Luke adds a detail that hearkens back to Elijah's resuscitation miracle: Jairus's daughter revives in much the same way as the Sidonian widow's son. In the son's case, "The life of the child returned to him [*epistrapsētō dē hē psychē tou paidariou toutou eis auton*]" (1 Kgs. 17:21). As for the daughter, "Her spirit returned [*kai epestrepsen to pneuma autēs*]" (Luke 8:55).

Now that Jesus has raised two dead children, the word is getting around. His reputation as a prophet has spread from Nain throughout Galilee. Even Herod has heard the rumor of Elijah's appearance. "Who is this about whom I hear such things?" he asks (Luke 9:8-9//Mark 6:15). Luke's audience is about to find out. In the next episode but one, Jesus asks his disciples, "Who do the crowds say that I am?" They report that that Jesus is thought to be Elijah. Jesus persists, "But who do you say that I am?" Peter's answer: "The Messiah of God" (Luke 9:18-20//Mark 8:27-29). Jesus may be a prophet like Elijah, but he is not the Elijah who heralds the day of the Lord. He is the Lord, the Messiah of God.

17. Luke also recapitulates other lines from Mark, such as "They were afraid," "They . . . glorified God" (Mark 5:15; 2:12; cf. Luke 7:16), and "I have compassion for the crowd" (Mark 8:2; cf. Luke 7:13).

18. Dabeck, "Siehe, es erschienen Moses und Elias," 181; Lampe, "Holy Spirit in the Writings of St Luke," 174–76; Hinnebusch, "Jesus, the New Elijah," 2178–79; Evans, "Luke's Use of the Elijah/Elisha Narratives," 79n22.

Luke continues to distinguish between Jesus and Elijah in a fourth scene, the account of Jesus' transfiguration (Luke 9:28-36//Mark 9:2-8). The scene takes place on a mountain (*oros*). Jesus appears in dazzling glory; Elijah appears with Jesus; in an echo of Ps. 2:7, a heavenly voice (*phonē*) says, "This is my Son." Once more, Luke reserves separate identities for Jesus and Elijah. The transfigured Jesus nevertheless resembles Elijah, the prophet who hears God's voice (*phonē*) on a mountain (*oros*; 1 Kgs. 19:8-18). Luke underscores the resemblance yet again when Jesus, coming down from the mountain, meets the father of a demon-possessed boy. As in the account of Jairus's daughter, Luke adds Elijah details to a story borrowed from Mark (Mark 9:14-29). According to Luke, the father informs Jesus, "He is my only child" (Luke 9:38). Luke then reports that Jesus, after healing the boy, "gave him back to his father [*kai apedōken auton tō patri autou*]" (Luke 9:42). The similarities to the Elijah story—and Luke's dead son story—are obvious.[19]

"Follow Me"

By the time Luke concludes his account of Jesus' Galilean ministry, he has compared Jesus to Elijah eight times. Jesus himself names Elijah as a precedent in his sermon at Nazareth. His wilderness sojourn, his encounter with God on a mountain, and his revival of three children confirm the likeness. Twice, Luke reports that some people identify Jesus as Elijah. Of course, Jesus is not Elijah, but—as Luke sees it—he is very much like Elijah.

Once we realize this, it is hard to miss the parallels that converge when Jesus ends his Galilean ministry and begins his journey to Jerusalem. The turning point comes in Luke 9:51: "When the days drew near for him to be taken up [*analēmpseōs*], he set his face to go to Jerusalem." Jesus speaks of his ascension, an event described only in Luke-Acts and often designated with the Greek verb *analambanein* (here and in Acts 1:2, 11, 22). By depicting Jesus' ascension in these terms, Luke stresses that Jesus' departure resembles that of Elijah, who was "taken up [*analēmphthēnai*]" into heaven (2 Kgs. 2:1-12).[20]

One might object to a proposed allusion based on a single similar verb, especially since Jesus does not leave the world exactly as Elijah has done. No chariot of fire appears; no whirlwind whisks Jesus away. Instead, he is "lifted up"

---

19. Compare Luke 9:38, 42 with 1 Kgs. 17:12, 23; Luke 7:12, 15. See also Johnson, *Gospel of Luke*, 158.

20. Dabeck, "Siehe, es erschienen Moses und Elias," 182; Hastings, *Prophet and Witness*, 72, 102; Evans, "Luke's Use of the Elijah/Elisha Narratives," 81; Johnson, *Gospel of Luke*, 162. The verb *analambanein* appears three times in 2 Kgs. 2:9-11.

into a cloud (Acts 1:9). This does not undermine the idea that Luke compares Jesus' ascension to Elijah's, however. It simply indicates that Luke is constrained by tradition. He cannot depict Jesus ascending in a whirlwind when he knows from Mark that the Messiah travels by cloud (Mark 13:26; 14:62). The argument for an allusion rests on other grounds: the verb *analambanein* plus the many Elijah allusions that precede and follow its first appearance. Because of these allusions, Luke's audience has already recognized Jesus as a prophet like Elijah before he announces that he will travel to Jerusalem. Like Elijah, he has raised a widow's only son, not to mention two other prostrate children. Now he will be "taken up."

Meanwhile, however, he has two Elijah-like interactions with his followers. These interactions set the stage for the apostles' ministry—first to Samaritans, then to Gentiles. They begin with Jesus already on his way to Jerusalem (Luke 9:52-56). The messengers who precede him enter a Samaritan village. The villagers, however, refuse to receive anyone in transit to Jerusalem. Their lack of hospitality, typical of first-century Jewish-Samaritan relations, prompts James and John to ask, "Lord, do you want us to command fire to come down from heaven and destroy them [*pyr katabēnai apo tou ouranou kai analōsai autous*]?" (Luke 9:54). Jesus, however, issues no such command. Instead, he rebukes James and John.[21]

Their question echoes an Elijah saying. Elijah twice gives the following order concerning Samaritan armies: "Let fire come down from heaven and consume you [*katabēsetai pyr ek tou ouranou kai kataphagetai se*]" (2 Kgs. 1:10, 12).[22] The heavenly fire obeys Elijah. Will Jesus, a prophet like Elijah, handle his Samaritan opponents in the same way? Absolutely not, says Luke. The time of final judgment has not yet arrived, not even for Samaritans who reject Jesus.[23]

Having spared Samaritans from heavenly fire, Luke goes on to rehabilitate them. First he shows that they are capable of righteous deeds. As Luke's Jesus sets out for Jerusalem, he tells the parable of the Good Samaritan (Luke 10:25-37). By loving his neighbor, this man fulfills one of the requirements for

---

21. The rebuke seems to have been borrowed from the rebuke of Peter in Mark 8:32-33 (missing from Luke 9, where it should appear between vv. 22 and 23). It apparently substitutes for the dispute with James and John in Mark 10:35-45 (also missing from between Luke 18:34 and 35).

22. Dabeck, "Siehe, es erschienen Moses und Elias," 182; Lampe, "Holy Spirit in the Writings of St Luke," 176; Hastings, *Prophet and Witness*, 72; Evans, "Luke's Use of the Elijah/Elisha Narratives," 80; Tannehill, *Narrative Unity of Luke-Acts*, 1:230; Johnson, *Gospel of Luke*, 162.

23. Another answer is given by a scribe whose addition first appears in fifth-century manuscripts. Jesus "has not come to destroy the lives of human beings but to save them." Hinnebusch gives a similar answer ("Jesus, the New Elijah," 2177).

inheriting eternal life. Then, toward the end of his journey, Jesus heals ten lepers (Luke 17:11-19). Luke patches the details together from some of Mark's healing stories: the lepers approach Jesus; they beg for mercy; they are made clean.[24] In an unexpected twist, however, only one of them—a Samaritan—returns to give thanks. Jesus tells him, "Your faith has made you well" (Luke 17:19).[25]

These stories lay the foundation for Acts 8:4-25, in which Samaria becomes a fertile mission field.[26] Philip makes so many converts there that Peter and John come from Jerusalem to lay their hands on them. Then, as Peter and John journey back to Jerusalem, they proclaim the good news in Samaritan villages. The Jewish Messiah's offer of salvation is extended and accepted among the northern tribes. Jesus may be a prophet like Elijah but not when it comes to destroying contrary Samaritans.

The final episode of Luke 9 lays the foundation for Gentile conversions. As Jesus continues on his way to Jerusalem, he begins a series of teachings by addressing some aspiring followers. "The Son of Man has nowhere to lay his head," he warns the first (Luke 9:58//Matt. 8:20). "Let the dead bury their own dead; but as for you, go and proclaim the kingdom of God," he tells the second (Luke 9:60//Matt. 8:22). To these two Q dialogues Luke adds a third. Another would-be disciple says, "I will follow you [akoloutheso soi], Lord; but let me first say farewell to those at my home." Jesus replies, "No one who puts a hand to the plow [arotron] and looks back is fit for the kingdom of God" (Luke 9:61-62).

Elijah receives a similar request from his protégé. Elisha is "plowing [ētoria]" when Elijah covers him with the prophet's mantle. "Let me kiss my father and my mother," says Elisha, "and then I will follow you [akoloutheso opisō sou]." Elijah wants nothing less than single-minded devotion, however, so Elisha sacrifices his oxen and follows Elijah (1 Kgs. 19:19-21).[27]

Like Elijah, Jesus prevents his followers from turning back even to bid their families farewell. Like Elisha, they must be wholly dedicated to his mission. Like Elisha, they receive their teacher's spirit after he is "taken up." And—just as Elijah went to a Sidonian widow and Elisha cleansed a Syrian leper—they bring good news to Gentiles. The lame walk, the dead are raised, and everyone who calls on the name of the Lord is saved.

---

24. Compare Luke 17:12-13 with Mark 5:2; 10:48; 1:42-44.

25. Luke borrows this pronouncement from Mark 5:34.

26. See also John T. Carroll, *Luke: A Commentary*, NTL (Louisville: Westminster John Knox, 2012), 229, 345.

27. Hastings, *Prophet and Witness*, 72; Hinnebusch, "Jesus, the New Elijah," 2237–39; Evans, "Luke's Use of the Elijah/Elisha Narratives," 81; Johnson, *Gospel of Luke*, 163.

5

A Rejected Prophet

Salvation is for everyone, says Luke—but not everyone accepted the offer. Jews in particular found it hard to believe in a messiah who had not saved them from Roman rule. Paul laments the fact in his letter written around 58 CE to believers in Rome: "I could wish that I myself were accursed and cut off from Christ for the sake of my own people. . . . My heart's desire and prayer to God for them is that they may be saved" (Rom. 9:3; 10:1). In Luke's day, Paul's prayer had not yet been answered. To be sure, many Jews did believe that Jesus was God's Anointed One. Nevertheless, the fact remained that their religious leaders had instigated his execution. In addition, most Jews—whom (according to Isa. 11:12) the Messiah was supposed to have gathered "from the four corners of the earth"—were still rejecting Jesus in large numbers.

Luke needs to explain this phenomenon.[1] He makes Jewish rejection one of the central themes of his two-volume work. He describes it; he accounts for it; he shows how it fulfills prophecy and is therefore—however unexpected—part of God's plan. In addition, Luke shows how the rejected Messiah was a prophet. In disputes, on trial, and with his last breath, Jesus utters oracles and discerns thoughts. He follows the precedent set by Scripture's rejected prophets.[2]

---

1. David L. Tiede, *Prophecy and History in Luke-Acts* (Philadelphia: Fortress Press, 1980), 120; Luke Timothy Johnson, *Luke-Acts: A Story of Prophet and People* (Chicago: Franciscan Herald, 1981), 21; Richard I. Pervo, *Acts: A Commentary*, Hermeneia (Minneapolis: Fortress Press, 2008), 23.

2. Robert C. Tannehill, *The Narrative Unity of Luke-Acts: A Literary Interpretation* (Philadelphia: Fortress Press, 1986), 1:96–99; Luke Timothy Johnson, *The Literary Function of Possessions in Luke-Acts*, SBLDS 39 (Missoula, MT: Scholars Press, 1977), 74–76; Johnson *Luke-Acts*, 27–29; Johnson, *The Acts of the Apostles*, SP 5 (Collegeville, MN: Liturgical, 1992), 13–14; Johnson, "The Christology of Luke-Acts," in *Who Do You Say That I Am? Essays on Christology*, ed. Mark Allan Powell and David R. Bauer (Louisville: Westminster John Knox, 1999), 56. Robert J. Karris takes a different view. He argues that the rejected-prophet theme highlights the grace and mercy of God, who (as in Neh. 9:26-31) continually sends prophets to a rebellious people (*Luke: Artist and Theologian: Luke's Passion Account as Literature* [New York: Paulist, 1985], 19–20).

There is no shortage of such prophets and the Israelites who reject them. They include Samuel and Elijah. King Saul disobeys Samuel not once but twice (1 Sam. 13:8-15; 15:10-31). King Ahab maligns Elijah; Queen Jezebel seeks to kill him (1 Kgs. 18:17; 19:2). Luke, however, does not stress the likeness of Samuel's or Elijah's rejection to the rejection of Jesus. He finds two more-useful precedents. One is Moses, Israel's lawgiver. Moses is an appropriate model because he foretold that God would raise up a prophet like himself (Deut. 18:15-22). For Luke, Jesus is that prophet: in touch with God, appointing leaders, rejected twice.[3] The other precedent is Jeremiah, Israel's quintessential rejected prophet. Like Jeremiah, Jesus prophesies against the temple, leading to his arrest and interrogation by Jerusalem officials. Together, Moses and Jeremiah offer compelling precedents. If Israel rejected important prophets like Moses and Jeremiah, then Luke's audience should not be surprised that so many Jews have rejected Jesus.

3. Many scholars note the parallels between Jesus and Moses discussed in this chapter. According to C. F. Evans, Adrian Hastings, and J. Severino Croatto, they identify Jesus as a kind of new Moses who delivers a new law (Evans, "The Central Section in St. Luke's Gospel," in *Studies in the Gospels*, ed. D. E. Nineham [Oxford: Blackwell, 1955], 42; Evans, *Saint Luke*, TPINTC [London: SCM, 1990], 70; Hastings, *A Prophet and Witness in Jerusalem: A Study of the Teaching of Saint Luke* [London: Longmans, Green, 1958], 74; Croatto, "Jesus, Prophet Like Elijah, and Prophet-Teacher Like Moses in Luke-Acts," *JBL* 124, no. 3 [2005]: 461). Gerhard Voss, Paul S. Minear, and Robert F. O'Toole emphasize Jesus' embodiment of various other characteristics of Moses. Jesus is the royal redeemer and prophetic mediator (Voss, *Die Christologie der lukanischen Schriften in Grundzügen*, StudNeot 2 [Paris: Desclée de Brouwer, 1965], 168); he is a redeemer and miracle-worker who delivers an urgent message (Minear, *To Heal and to Reveal: The Prophetic Vocation According to Luke* [New York: Seabury, 1976], 105–8); he is the eschatological prophet who brings salvation, fulfills God's promises, pastors his people, suffers, and calls Israel to listen (O'Toole, "The Parallels between Jesus and Moses," *BTB* 20 [1990]: 28; O'Toole, *Luke's Presentation of Jesus: A Christology*, SubBi 25 [Rome: Editrice Pontificio Istituto Biblico, 2004], 52). Scholars who highlight Moses' rejection by Israel include Howard M. Teeple, Luke Timothy Johnson, Tiede, David P. Moessner, Jerome Neyrey, and D. A. S. Ravens (see Teeple, *The Mosaic Eschatological Prophet*, SBLMS 10 [Philadelphia: Society of Biblical Literature, 1957], 86–87; Johnson, *Literary Function of Possessions*, 125; Johnson, *Luke-Acts*, 21–29; Johnson, *The Gospel of Luke*, SP 3 [Collegeville, MN: Liturgical, 1991], 18–20; Johnson, "Christology of Luke-Acts," 56–59; Tiede, *Prophecy and History in Luke-Acts*, 40–42; Moessner, "Paul and the Pattern of the Prophet Like Moses in Acts," in *SBL 1983 Seminar Papers*, ed. Kent H. Richards, SBLSP 22 [Chico, CA: Scholars Press, 1983], 206; Moessner, *Lord of the Banquet: The Literary and Theological Significance of the Lukan Travel Narrative* [Minneapolis: Fortress Press, 1989], 46, 60–68, 84; Neyrey, *The Passion According to Luke: A Redaction Study of Luke's Soteriology* [New York: Paulist, 1985], 94; Ravens, "Luke 9.7-62 and the Prophetic Role of Jesus," *NTS* 36 [1990]: 121–23, 128).

"You Rejected the Holy and Righteous One"

In many ways, Luke's story is a story of Jewish acceptance. Jesus gains Jewish disciples and sways Jewish crowds.[4] Thousands of Jews receive the good news proclaimed by the apostles.[5] For the most part, however, Luke stresses Jewish rejection. Building on episodes from Mark and Q, he constructs a narrative in which Jews and especially Jewish leaders refuse God's salvation twice: first as offered by Jesus and John the Baptist; the second time as offered by Peter and Paul.

Their refusal is based on three issues: Gentile inclusion, forgiveness of sins, and Sabbath observance. The first becomes apparent in the paradigmatic scene at the synagogue in Nazareth. Here, the congregation mistreats Jesus only after he compares himself to Elijah and Elisha, sent by God to a Sidonian widow and a Syrian leper (Luke 4:25-30). It is hard for them to believe that the Anointed One would offer God's salvation to uncircumcised Gentiles.

This is the only time in Luke's Gospel that Jews reject Jesus because of Gentile inclusion. There are more such instances in Acts.[6] Meanwhile, Jewish leaders oppose Jesus on other grounds—grounds laid out in the five controversy stories of Mark 2:1—3:6. Luke reiterates these stories, adding similar episodes to highlight the relevant issues. How can the Messiah forgive sinners? How can he break the Sabbath?

The controversy over sinners begins with Mark's stories of the paralytic and the dinner at Levi's house. The Pharisees clearly state their concerns: "Who can forgive sins but God alone?" "Why do you eat and drink with tax collectors and sinners?" (Luke 5:21, 30//Mark 2:7, 16). By forgiving the paralytic, Jesus has committed blasphemy. By eating with tax collectors and sinners, Jesus has made himself ritually impure.

Similar disputes flare up throughout Jesus' ministry.[7] At dinner with Simon the Pharisee, Jesus allows the sinful woman to anoint his feet. "She is a sinner," thinks Simon (Luke 7:39). When Jesus goes on to forgive the woman, the dinner guests murmur, "Who is this who even forgives sins?" (Luke 7:49). Their opposition does not stop Jesus from associating with sinners as he makes his way to Jerusalem. "This fellow welcomes sinners and eats with them," grumble the scribes and Pharisees—giving rise to the parables of the Lost Sheep, the Lost Coin, and the Prodigal Son (Luke 15:1-32). When Jesus stays with the chief tax

---

4. Luke 4:42—5:11; 5:15; 6:12-19; 8:1-4, 40; 9:10-11, 37; 12:1; 14:25; 19:37-38; 23:50-53.

5. Acts 1:15; 2:41; 4:4; 5:14; 6:7; 9:31; 13:43; 14:1; 15:5; 17:4, 12; 18:8; 28:24.

6. Acts 13:45-50; 17:4-5; 21:27-30; 22:21-22.

7. See also Tannehill, *Narrative Unity of Luke-Acts*, 1:171–99.

collector Zacchaeus, everyone is shocked: "He has gone to be the guest of one who is a sinner" (Luke 19:7).

To these five disputes about sinners, Luke adds four Sabbath controversies. Again, he borrows the first two from Mark: the disciples pluck heads of grain and Jesus heals a man with a withered hand. "Why are you doing what is not lawful on the sabbath?" ask the Pharisees (Luke 6:2//Mark 2:24). They watch to see whether he will heal the man and break the law (Luke 6:7//Mark 3:2). They continue to watch through two more Sabbath episodes found only in Luke, as Jesus heals a crippled woman and a man with dropsy (Luke 13:10-17; 14:1-6).

The Pharisees simply cannot accept that a blaspheming, impure Sabbath breaker is Israel's Messiah. They cannot understand that this is why Jesus and his disciples do not fast (Luke 5:33-39//Mark 2:18-22). They think he has a demon; they ask for a sign (Luke 11:15-16//Mark 3:22; 8:11-13). In return, Jesus accuses them of hypocrisy and greed (Luke 11:39-52//Matt. 23:4-36; Luke 20:45-47//Mark 12:38-40). He goes on to confront the Jerusalem establishment, driving merchants out of the temple and blaming them for mismanagement (Luke 19:45-46; 20:9-19//Mark 11:15-17; 12:1-12). He alienates Pharisees and Sadducees, chief priests and scribes. They keep looking for ways to accuse him of a capital offense (Luke 6:7, 11//Mark 3:2, 6; Luke 11:53-54; Luke 19:47//Mark 11:18).

When the chief priests, scribes, and elders finally bring Jesus before Pilate, they say nothing about blasphemy, impurity, or Sabbath breaking. Instead, they charge him according to Roman law: "We found this man perverting our nation, forbidding us to pay taxes to the emperor, and saying that he himself is the Messiah, a king" (Luke 23:2). Because it is important for Luke that Pilate should find Jesus innocent of breaking Roman law, Luke's Pilate exonerates Jesus three times (Luke 23:4, 14, 22). Luke even has Pilate send Jesus to Herod Antipas, who agrees that Jesus is innocent (Luke 23:6-12, 15). Pilate finally condemns Jesus not because Jesus is guilty but because of pressure from "the chief priests, the leaders, and the people" (Luke 23:13). Luke underscores their influence with three additions to Mark's trial narrative. When the people demand a second time that Jesus be crucified, Luke notes that "their voices prevailed" (Luke 23:23). Pilate gives sentence, not that the penalty of the law should be carried out, but "that their demand should be granted" (Luke 23:24). He hands Jesus over "as they wished" (Luke 23:25).[8]

As Luke depicts opposition from Jews, he comments on the trend. In the Gospel, he inserts an editorial aside into a John-the-Baptist episode from Q. Jesus, explaining John's identity and mission, quotes Mal. 3:1 to imply that John

---

8. Ibid., 1:198. Compare Luke 23:23-25 with Mark 15:14-15.

is the Messiah's herald: "This is the one about whom it is written, 'See, I am sending my messenger ahead of you, who will prepare your way before you'" (Luke 7:27//Matt 11:10). Luke adds this remark: "And all the people who heard this, including the tax collectors, acknowledged the justice of God, because they had been baptized with John's baptism. But by refusing to be baptized by him, the Pharisees and the lawyers rejected God's purpose for themselves" (Luke 7:29-30).[9]

In Acts, Luke extends the indictment to the Jerusalem establishment. Peter and Stephen consistently accuse Jerusalem Jews of crucifying the Messiah (Acts 2:22-23; 4:10-11; 5:30; 7:52). The most detailed accusation comes from Peter's second speech in Acts: "The God of Abraham, the God of Isaac, and the God of Jacob, the God of our ancestors has glorified his servant Jesus, whom you handed over and rejected in the presence of Pilate, though he had decided to release him. But you rejected the Holy and Righteous One and asked to have a murderer given to you, and you killed the Author of life, whom God raised from the dead" (Acts 3:13-15). From the Pharisees and lawyers to the chief priests, leaders, and people, Jews consistently reject their Messiah. In doing so, says Luke, they deny the Holy and Righteous One. They kill the Author of life. They reject God's purpose for themselves.

"What the Prophets Said"

Having acknowledged this anomaly, Luke must now account for it. He does so in part by showing how it fulfills prophecy. He cites three passages from Israel's Scriptures that, in his view, indicate that Jewish rejection of God's Messiah was foretold by Israel's prophets. As the narrative progresses, Simeon and Jesus weigh in with prophecies of what will soon take place. All these prophecies indicate what Peter explains in his first speech: that Jesus was handed over to his Jewish opponents "by the definite plan and foreknowledge of God" (Acts 2:23).[10]

Simeon is the first prophet in Luke's story to foresee Jewish rejection. After proclaiming Jesus as God's salvation, "a light for revelation to the Gentiles and for glory to [God's] people Israel," Simeon tells Mary that the "child is destined for the falling and the rising of many in Israel, and to be a sign that will be opposed" (Luke 2:29-34). While God's Messiah is still a babe in arms, one of the first prophets to recognize him warns that not all Jews will follow suit.[11]

9. This remark may be loosely based on another Q passage (cf. Matt. 21:31-32).
10. God's plan is also stressed in Acts 3:13-18, 27-28.
11. Johnson, *Literary Function of Possessions*, 91; Johnson, *Luke-Acts*, 32.

A second prophecy of rejection comes from Israel's Scriptures. Luke introduces it when Jesus tells the parable of the Sower. In this parable, borrowed from Mark, a man scatters seeds on various kinds of soil. When the disciples request an interpretation, Jesus cites Isa. 6:9. He tells parables so that

> looking [*blepontes*] they may not perceive,
>   and listening [*akouontes*] they may not understand. (Luke 8:10//Mark 4:12)

Mark 4:12 continues with Isa. 6:10: "so that they may not turn again and be forgiven."[12] Luke, however, continues by showing how the parable itself illustrates the quotation. "The seed is the word of God," explains Jesus, and the path represents "those who have heard [*akousantes*]; then the devil comes and takes away the word from their hearts" (Luke 8:11-12//Mark 4:14-15). Luke then adds a paraphrase of Isa. 6:10: "so that they may not believe and be saved" (Luke 8:12).[13] The parable of the Sower, along with Isaiah's prophecy, effectively explains the Pharisees' response to Jesus. Although they hear God's word, they cannot understand it. It bounces off them like seeds hitting a dirt path.

When Jesus begins his journey to Jerusalem, the prophecies begin to focus on what will happen there. Luke's Jesus flexes his prophetic muscles by issuing six predictions of his suffering, death, and resurrection: three from Mark's Gospel (Luke 9:22, 44; 18:31-33//Mark 8:31; 9:31; 10:33-34), one from Q (Luke 13:32-33//Matt 23:37), and two added by Luke (Luke 12:50; 17:25).[14] The first prediction, copied from Mark, names the instigators: "the elders, chief priests, and scribes." The fourth, based on an oracle from Q, names the place: "Jerusalem."

Along the journey, Luke's Jesus delivers more Q oracles about Jewish rejection and its consequences. He warns townspeople and villagers that although prophets, patriarchs, and people from all over will enter the kingdom of God, they themselves are likely to be thrown out (Luke 13:28-29//Matt. 8:11-12). He reinforces this point in the parable of the Great Dinner, explaining

---

12. New Testament use of Isa. 6:9-10 is not limited to the Synoptic Gospels. John also cites these verses as a prophecy of the effect that Jesus' signs had on his own people (John 12:39-40). See also Pervo, *Acts*, 685.

13. He replaces "turn again and be forgiven" with "believe and be saved," introducing language that he will use over and over in Acts (Acts 4:4, 12; 9:42; 10:43; 11:17, 21; 13:12, 39, 48; 14:1, 23; 15:7, 11; 16:31; 17:12, 34; 18:8).

14. See also Hastings, *Prophet and Witness*, 65; Johnson, *Luke-Acts*, 35; Johnson, *Gospel of Luke*, 381.

that this is because they have refused God's invitation (Luke 14:15-24//Matt. 22:1-10). His fifth passion prediction, found only in Luke, drives the point home: "[The Son of Man] must endure much suffering and be rejected by this generation" (Luke 17:25). Here Luke identifies Jesus' persecutors as "this generation," a phrase used by Mark and Q to refer to unbelieving Jews.[15]

Luke illustrates the Messiah's rejection by Jerusalem authorities with the parable of the Wicked Tenants (Luke 20:9-19//Mark 12:1-12). Like the parable of the Sower, the parable of the Wicked Tenants originates with Mark. It, too, features a prophecy about Jewish rejection taken from Israel's Scriptures. While teaching in the temple, Jesus tells the story of the tenants of a vineyard who refuse to give the owner his rightful share, killing the servants who come to claim it. When they kill his son, the vineyard owner destroys the tenants and replaces them. "Heaven forbid!" cries Jesus' audience. Jesus refers them to Ps. 118:22:

> The stone that the builders rejected
>   has become the cornerstone. (Luke 20:17//Mark 12:10)

The temple authorities understand that they are the parable's "tenants." They are the prophecy's "builders." They have rejected God's prophets, and they are about to reject God's Son. After they have Jesus crucified, Peter once again reminds them of Ps. 118:22:

> The stone that was rejected by you, the builders;
>   it has become the cornerstone. (Acts 4:11)

The added second-person pronoun makes it clear: Ps. 118:22 refers to the Jewish leaders who condemned the Messiah and handed him over for execution.

There is one more prophecy that Luke applies explicitly to Jewish rejection of Jesus. That prophecy is Ps. 2:1-2:

> Why did the Gentiles rage,
>   and the peoples imagine vain things?
> The kings of the earth took their stand,
>   and the rulers have gathered together
> against the Lord and against his Messiah. (Acts 4:25-26)

---

15. Mark 8:12; Mark 9:19; Matt 11:16//Luke 7:31; Matt 12:39-42//Luke 11:29-32; Matt 23:36//Luke 11:50-51. Possibly this phrase comes from Isa. 53:8 (LXX), quoted in Acts 8:33.

According to Luke, the "king" is the Jewish ethnarch Herod Antipas and the "peoples" are "the Gentiles and the people of Israel" (Acts 4:27). God's plan for the Messiah who will break the nations "with a rod of iron, and dash them in pieces like a potter's vessel" (Ps. 2:9) therefore includes rejection by Jews.

"A Prophet Mighty in Deed and Word"

It does not seem to have been enough for Luke to stress prophecies of Jewish rejection. He also highlights the fact that the rejected Messiah is a prophet. As Luke's Jesus argues with his opponents and goes to his death, he delivers prophetic oracles and demonstrates prophetic knowledge. Luke also compares Jewish rejection of Jesus to Israel's rejection of other prophets.[16] In this way, he assures his audience that Jewish rejection of the Messiah is not so surprising after all. Israel has always rejected God's prophets.

Three of Luke's rejected-prophet episodes appear in his account of Jesus in Galilee. The first is the paradigmatic scene in the synagogue at Nazareth, taken from Mark. "No prophet is accepted in the prophet's hometown," prophesies Jesus. The people of his hometown fulfill that prophecy by rejecting him (Luke 4:24-30//Mark 6:1-6). In his next sermon, borrowed from Q, Luke's Jesus tells his disciples, "Blessed are you when people hate you, and when they exclude you, revile you, and defame you on account of the Son of Man. Rejoice in that day and leap for joy, for surely your reward is great in heaven; for that is what their ancestors did to the prophets" (Luke 6:22-23//Matt. 5:11-12).[17] Jesus has a reason to take his own advice at Simon the Pharisee's dinner. Simon is disposed to reject Jesus, the prophet who reads his mind, tells him a parable, and knows all about the foot-washing woman's sins (Luke 7:39-48).

As he travels to Jerusalem, Luke's Jesus expands on three Q sayings to connect his own rejection with the rejection of Israel's prophets. First, he offers the crowds a sign: the sign of Jonah (Luke 11:29-32//Matt. 12:38-42). For Matthew, the sign is Jonah's three days in the fish's belly. For Luke, the sign is Jonah's judgment oracle: "Forty days more, and Nineveh will be overthrown!" (Jon. 3:4). "The people of Nineveh will rise up at the judgment with this generation and condemn it," says Luke's Jesus, "because they repented at the proclamation of Jonah, and see, something greater than Jonah is here!" (Luke 11:32). For Luke, "this generation" is worse even than Nineveh, that archetypal wicked city. Nineveh accepted Jonah, but "this generation" rejects an even greater prophet—Jesus.[18]

---

16. Henry J. Cadbury, *The Making of Luke-Acts*, 3rd ed. (Peabody, MA: Hendrickson, 1999), 256–57.

17. Johnson, *Literary Function of Possessions*, 91–96; Tannehill, *Narrative Unity of Luke-Acts*, 1:72–73.

Jesus goes on to pronounce woes on Pharisees and lawyers, accusing them (among other things) of complicity in the murder of Israel's prophets (Luke 11:47-51//Matt. 23:29-36). Since they built the prophets' tombs, they witness and approve the deeds of their ancestors. Accordingly, Jesus issues a warning: "Therefore also the Wisdom of God said, 'I will send them prophets and apostles, some of whom they will kill and persecute'" (Luke 11:49). This warning has terrible implications. When the Pharisees and lawyers kill and persecute Jesus and his followers, they not only witness and approve the deeds of their ancestors—they also perform those deeds. They kill God's prophets.[19]

The series ends with a lament over Jerusalem, taken from Q. Luke's Jesus introduces the lament with the striking observation that "it is impossible for a prophet to be killed outside of Jerusalem" (Luke 13:33). With this statement, Luke points to Jerusalem's reputation for rejecting prophets like Jesus. He follows through with this Q saying: "Jerusalem, Jerusalem, the city that kills the prophets and stones those who are sent to it! How often I have desired to gather your children together as a hen gathers her brood under her wings, and you were not willing" (Luke 13:34//Matt. 23:37). The city that kills the prophets is about to kill Jesus.[20]

In the end, Jerusalem kills Luke's Jesus because of a prophetic action: he ejects merchants from the temple (Luke 19:45-46//Mark 11:15-17). Luke's Jesus follows this prophetic action with the parable of the Wicked Tenants (Luke 20:9-15//Mark 12:1-12). The parable stresses that the tenants reject their landlord's son just as they have previously rejected the landlord's servants. In other words, the chief priests and scribes will kill Jesus just as their ancestors killed the prophets. When they do arrest Jesus, Luke makes it clear that they are persecuting a prophet. As his custodians beat him and insult him, they mock his prophetic ability by blindfolding him and saying, "Prophesy! Who is it that struck you?" (Luke 22:63-65//Mark 14:65). Ironically, this fulfills one of Jesus' prophecies: "[The Son of Man] will be mocked and insulted and spat upon" (Luke 18:32//Mark 10:34). It is worth noting that while Mark's prediction says that the Gentiles will mock, insult, and spit upon Jesus, Luke's prediction never specifies the agent. Unlike Mark's Pilate, Luke's Pilate never has Jesus flogged.[21] All the mistreatment comes from Jews.

18. See also Johnson, *Gospel of Luke*, 187.

19. See also G. W. H. Lampe, "The Holy Spirit in the Writings of St Luke," in *Studies in the Gospels*, ed. D. E. Nineham (Oxford: Blackwell, 1955), 173; Tannehill, *Narrative Unity of Luke-Acts*, 1:182.

20. See also Lampe, "Holy Spirit in the Writings of St Luke"; Hastings, *Prophet and Witness*, 108; Minear, *To Heal and to Reveal*, 103; Johnson, *Luke-Acts*, 35.

21. Compare Luke 23:1-25 with Mark 15:1-15.

As he goes to his death, Luke's Jesus continues to prophesy. On the way to Calvary, he warns Jerusalem's women of the depredations to come (Luke 23:26-31). Crucified between two criminals, he suffers one last rejection. "Are you not the Messiah?" one of them asks. "Save yourself and us!" (Luke 23:39). He also delivers one last prediction, telling the other, "Today you will be with me in Paradise" (Luke 23:43). All this fits Cleopas's summary: Jesus was "a prophet mighty in deed and word before God and all the people" whom "our chief priests and leaders handed . . . over to be condemned to death and crucified" (Luke 24:19-20).[22]

"Listen to Him!"

As we have seen, Luke goes out of his way to portray Jesus as a prophet, rejected as were the prophets of old. A closer reading of Luke-Acts indicates that he seems to have two specific prophets in mind. One of them is Israel's greatest prophet, Moses. Two explicit references in Peter's and Stephen's speeches clarify the points of comparison. First, Moses is rejected twice: once by the Hebrew laborer whom he saves from a beating; a second time by the Israelites who sacrifice to a golden calf after he has saved them from Pharaoh (Acts 7:23-41). Second, Jesus is the prophet like Moses foretold in Deuteronomy: "The Lord your God will raise up [*anastēsei*] a prophet like me from your people. You shall listen [*akousesthe*] to him. . . . I will raise [*anastēsō*] up for them a prophet like you from among their kinsfolk; I will put my words in his mouth, and he will speak to them just as I command him. And anyone who does not listen [*akousē*] to whatever the prophet speaks in my name, I myself will punish that person" (Deut. 18:15, 18-19; cf. Acts 3:22-23; 7:37). These are powerful precedents for Luke. They allow him to show how God vindicates Jesus—like Moses, rejected by his own people—making him the people's ruler and liberator. They allow him to portray a second rejection—this time, a rejection of Jesus' apostles—as a matter of course (Acts 7:35).[23] They allow him to insinuate that if the people do not listen to Jesus—the prophet like Moses—God will punish them (Acts 3:23).[24]

As important as these explicit references are, Luke does not lead off with them. He leads up to them, starting in the Gospel narrative with a series of implicit comparisons. Luke follows Mark by showing that, like Moses, Jesus spends forty days in the wilderness (Luke 4:1-2//Mark 1:12-13; cf. Exod. 24:18;

---

22. See also Johnson, *Literary Function of Possessions*, 83–84.

23. Johnson, *Luke-Acts*, 24–29.

24. Hastings, *Prophet and Witness*, 95–96; Tiede, *Prophecy and History in Luke-Acts*, 40; Donald Juel, *Luke-Acts: The Promise of History* (Atlanta: John Knox, 1983), 45–46, 110.

34:28; Deut. 9:9) and gathers twelve followers (Luke 6:13-16//Mark 3:13-19; cf. Num. 1:5-15). In the transfiguration scene, Luke stresses the likeness with references to the events at Mount Sinai. He changes Mark's story by reporting that Jesus "went up [*anebē*]" on a "mountain [*oros*]" (Luke 9:28; cf. Exod. 19:20) to speak about his "departure [*exodon*]" (Luke 9:31; cf. Exod. 19:1).[25] To Mark's account of God's voice from the "cloud [*nephelēs*]," Luke adds that the disciples—like the Israelites at Sinai—"were afraid [*ephobēthēsan*]" (Luke 9:34-35; cf. Exod. 19:9; 20:18).[26] The voice's exhortation, "Listen [*akouete*] to him," is reminiscent of Deut. 18:15 (Luke 9:35//Mark 9:7). When people declare that Jesus is one of the ancient prophets, Luke adds that the prophet has "arisen [*anestē*]" (Luke 9:8, 19), apparently alluding to Deut. 18:15, 18.[27]

As Jesus begins his journey to Jerusalem, Luke continues to show that he is the prophet like Moses. "He sent messengers ahead of him [*apesteilen angelous*]," writes Luke, implying the fulfillment of God's promise to Moses: "I am sending my messenger ahead of you [*egō apostellō ton angelon mou pro prosōpou sou*]" (Luke 9:52; cf. Exod. 23:20).[28] He then appoints seventy followers just as Moses appointed seventy elders (Luke 10:1; cf. Num. 11:16).[29] Already there are hints that Israel will reject this prophet like Moses. A Samaritan village refuses to receive him (Luke 9:52-53); Galilean towns will not repent (Luke 10:13-16//Matt. 11:20-24). Still, Jesus continues to heal the lame, the deaf, the lepers, and the blind—performing "deeds of power, wonders, and signs [*sēmeia kai terata*]" as did Moses (Acts 2:22; cf. Deut. 34:11).[30]

---

25. Compare Luke 9:28, 31 with Mark 9:2, 4.

26. Compare Luke 9:34-35 with Mark 9:7.

27. Compare Luke 9:8, 19 to Mark 6:15; 8:28.

28. Luke 9:52 is reminiscent of Mark 1:2: "See, I am sending my messenger ahead of you [*apostellō ton angelon mou pro prosōpou sou*], who will prepare your way." The expression conflates Exod. 23:20 with Mal. 3:1: "See, I am sending my messenger [*exapostellō ton angelon mou*] to prepare the way before me [*pro prosōpou mou*]." Luke seems to have moved the expression from Mark's prophecy about John the Baptist (Mark 1:2-3; cf. Luke 3:4-6) to a description of Jesus at the beginning of his journey to Jerusalem. The new placement may have something to do with the fact that in both Mal. 3:1 and Luke 9:52-57 the "Lord" (*kyrios*) is on his "way" (*hodos*) to the temple (cf. Luke 19:45). See also Paul Hinnebusch, "Jesus, the New Elijah, in Saint Luke," *TBT* 31 (1967): 2178.

29. While Codex Sinaiticus reports that Jesus appointed seventy others, Codex Alexandrinus and Codex Vaticanus make it seventy-two. The latter number might symbolize the seventy-two nations of the earth as enumerated in the LXX. The number seventy, however, more closely coheres with Luke's intention elsewhere to portray Jesus as a prophet like Moses (see also Johnson, *Gospel of Luke*, 167). For a discussion of the variant, see Bruce M. Metzger, *A Textual Commentary on the Greek New Testament* (Stuttgart: United Bible Societies, 1971), 150.

The first explicit reference to Deut. 18:15, 18-19 occurs in Peter's second speech. First, Peter offers a direct (if somewhat altered) quotation. "Moses said, 'The Lord your God will raise up [anastēsei] for you from your own people a prophet like me,'" says Peter. "You must listen to whatever he tells you. And it will be that everyone who does not listen to that prophet will be utterly rooted out of the people" (Acts 3:22-23). In chapter 8, we will examine Luke's modification to Deut. 18:19. For now, we should note the end of Peter's speech: "When God raised up [anastēsas] his servant, he sent him first to you" (Acts 3:26). There can be no doubt the resurrected Jesus is the prophet whom God raised up. He is the prophet like Moses.

Stephen's speech spells out the precise similarities by recapitulating Moses' story. Stephen begins by introducing Moses, who "was instructed in all the wisdom of the Egyptians and was powerful in his words and deeds" (Acts 7:22). He continues to relate how Moses visited "his relatives, the Israelites" (Acts 7:23) and defended a Hebrew laborer from his oppressor. The next day, when Moses attempted to settle a dispute, the quarreling Hebrews resented his interference. Stephen offers this interpretation: "[Moses] supposed that his kinsfolk understood that God was giving them salvation through him, but they did not understand" (Acts 7:25, my translation). They pushed Moses aside.[31]

Stephen does not tell this familiar tale simply to entertain his audience. He tells it to make an important point: the story of Moses is the story of Jesus. Like Moses, Jesus was instructed in wisdom (Luke 2:40, 52), powerful in word and deed (Luke 24:19). Like Moses, Jesus was giving salvation to Israel, but they did not understand (Luke 23:35-37). They rejected Jesus just as they rejected Moses.[32]

"IF I TELL YOU, YOU WILL NOT BELIEVE"

The parallels between Jesus and Moses tend to illustrate the significance of Jesus' rejection: his opponents listen but do not understand. With regard to the specific details, however, Jesus is more like Jeremiah: his opponents do

---

30. Johnson, *Literary Function of Possessions*, 61; Johnson, *Luke-Acts*, 27. Moses is said to perform "signs" in Exod. 4:8-9, 17, 28, 30 and "wonders" in Exod. 3:20; 4:21; 11:10. In Exod. 8:23; 10:1-2, God performs "signs"; in Exod. 11:9; 15:11, God does "wonders." According to Exod. 7:3; Pss. 78:43; 135:9; Jer. 32:20-21, God performs "signs and wonders." Psalm 105:27 sums it up: Moses and Aaron performed God's "signs" and "wonders."

31. Acts 7:22-29; cf. Exod 2:11-22.

32. Lampe, "Holy Spirit in the Writings of St Luke," 175; Hastings, *Prophet and Witness*, 69; F. F. Bruce, *Commentary on the Book of Acts* (London: Marshall, Morgan & Scott, 1954), 151; Johnson, *Luke-Acts*, 27–29.

not listen. Instead, they arrest him and interrogate him because of his pronouncements concerning the Jerusalem temple.

The comparison begins in Jesus' journey to Jerusalem as he echoes prophecies, mostly from Jeremiah, about the Holy City. The first echo sounds in his declaration of woe to Pharisees and lawyers whose ancestors murdered the prophets. We have seen how Jesus warns them that when they kill God's prophets and apostles, they perform their ancestors' deeds. Presently, we will see how Jesus predicts that they will be charged with murdering all the prophets. Meanwhile, we must pay attention to the scriptural allusions in Jesus' indictment: "Therefore also the Wisdom of God said, 'I will send them prophets and apostles [apostelō eis autous prophētas kai apostolous], some of whom they will kill and persecute,' so that this generation may be charged with the blood of all the prophets shed since the foundation of the world, from the blood of Abel to the blood of Zechariah, who perished between the altar and the sanctuary" (Luke 11:47-51). There are at least three allusive referents. Two are from Jeremiah:

> From the day that their ancestors came out of the land of Egypt even until this day, I sent to you [exapesteila pros hymas] all my servants the prophets [prophētas]. I sent them day after day but they did not listen [ouk ēkousan] to me; they did not incline their ear and they stiffened their necks even more than their ancestors did. So you will speak to them this word: "This is the nation that did not listen [ouk ēkousen] to the voice of the Lord." (Jer. 7:25-28)

> Although I sent to you [apestellon pros hymas] my servants the prophets [prophētas] early in the morning, you neither listened [ouk eisēkousate] nor inclined your ear. (Jer. 25:4)[33]

A similar passage is found in 2 Chronicles:

> He sent to them prophets [apesteilen pros autous prophētas] to turn them to the Lord but they did not listen [ouk ēkousan]. They warned them but they did not listen [ouk ēkousan]. (2 Chron. 24:19)

This last referent reverberates loudest with Jesus' indictment simply because it precedes the story of the rejected prophet Zechariah son of Jehoiada, stoned to death in the temple court by order of King Joash.[34] The Jeremiah texts add

33. See also Hastings, *Prophet and Witness*, 117.

resonance to the idea that God sent prophets to people who did not listen. Moreover, all three passages share vocabulary with prophecies quoted elsewhere in Luke-Acts. These include the predictions of a prophet like Moses:

> The Lord your God will raise up [*anastēsei*] a prophet like me from your people. You shall listen [*akousesthe*] to him. . . . I will raise [*anastēsō*] up for them a prophet [*prophētēn*] like you from among their kinsfolk; I will put my words in his mouth, and he will speak to them just as I command him. And anyone who does not listen [*akousē*] to whatever the prophet [*prophētēs*] speaks in my name, I myself will punish that person. (Deut. 18:15, 18-19; cf. Acts 3:22-23; 7:37)

They also include Isaiah's commission:

> Keep listening [*akoē akousete*], but do not understand;
>> keep looking, but do not perceive. (Isa. 6:9; cf. Luke 8:10; Acts 28:26)

Overall, these passages send a consistent message: God always sends prophets but Israel never listens.

A second allusion responds to a report from some bystanders about Pilate's violent retribution against some Galileans. To this report, Jesus adds a second object lesson: Jerusalemites crushed by a falling tower. He warns, "Unless you repent [*ean mē metanoēte*], you will all perish [*apoleisthe*] as they did" (Luke 13:1-5). Jesus refers to the coming sieges in Galilee and Jerusalem, evoking one of Jeremiah's oracles: "Unless they turn back [*ean de mē epistrepsōsin*], I will remove [them] with destruction and annihilation [*apōleia*]" (Jer. 12:17).

Luke's Jesus follows this Jeremiah-like warning with a Jeremiah-like illustration. He tells a parable about a vineyard owner who wants to get rid of his unproductive fig tree (*sykē*). The situation is reminiscent of Jeremiah's accusation against Jerusalem's scribes: "There are no grapes on the vines; there are no figs on the fig trees [*sykais*]; even the leaves have fallen off" (Jer. 8:13). When Luke's vineyard owner orders his gardener to "cut it down," the gardener replies, "Let it alone for one more year, until I dig around it and put manure on it. If it bears fruit next year, well and good; but if not, you can cut it down"

---

34. See 2 Chron. 24:20-22. Greek versions give the prophet's name as Azariah. Luke follows Q in basing the name on the Hebrew text.

(Luke 13:6-9). Jesus, like Jeremiah, gives the people of Jerusalem a chance to repent.

More Jeremiah oracles resonate in Jesus' two laments. To the first lament, borrowed from Q, Luke adds this warning: "Your house is left [*aphietai hymin ho oikos*] to you" (Luke 13:35; cf. Matt 23:38). In the second lament, found only in Luke, Jesus weeps (*eklausen*) over the Holy City. He can see the coming siege in his mind's eye. "If you, even you had only recognized [*egnōs*] on this day the things that make for peace [*eirēnēn*]!" he wails. He then levels this accusation: "You did not recognize the time of your visitation [*ouk egnōs ton kairon tēs episkopēs sou*]" (Luke 19:41-44).

Jeremiah is only other prophet to mourn over Jerusalem in this way. "I have forsaken my house [*ton oikon mou*]," he cries, speaking for God; "I have left [*aphēka*] my inheritance" (Jer. 12:7). This makes him want to "weep [*klausomai*] day and night" for his people (Jer. 9:1). Because they said, "Peace, peace [*eirēnē, eirēnē*]" when there was no peace and "did not know [*ouk egnōsan*]" their shame, says Jeremiah, "they will perish in the time of their visitation [*en kairō episkopēs*]" (Jer. 6:14-15).[35]

Luke's Jesus imitates Jeremiah most explicitly when he enters the temple and begins to drive out the merchants (Luke 19:45-46//Mark 11:15-17). Here Jesus performs a prophetic action.[36] This particular prophetic action illustrates a judgment oracle drawn from Israel's prophets. First, Isaiah lays out God's commandment: "My house shall be a house of prayer" (Luke 11:46; cf. Isa. 56:7). Then, from his famous "temple sermon," Jeremiah provides the accusation: "You have made it a den of robbers" (Luke 11:46; cf. Jer. 7:11). For Luke, as for Mark, this is Jesus' "temple sermon." It leads to predictions of the Roman siege—predictions borrowed from Mark and expanded by Luke. Luke's additions allude to several prophetic oracles, among them the judgment oracles of Jeremiah. For Luke, the days of the siege are "days of vengeance [*hēmerai ekdikēseōs*]" like the "day of vengeance [*hēmera ekdikēseōs*]" pronounced by Jeremiah on the Lord's enemies (Luke 21:22; cf. Jer. 46:10).[37] "There will be great distress on the land [*epi tēs gēs*]" as in the days when God brought the Babylonians "against this land [*epi tēn gēn tautēn*]" (Luke 21:23, my translation;

---

35. See also Hastings, *Prophet and Witness*, 118.

36. Other scholars who recognize Luke 19:45-46 as a prophetic action include Joel B. Green, John Nolland, and O'Toole (see Green, *The Gospel of Luke*, NICNT [Grand Rapids: Eerdmans, 1997], 692; Nolland, *Luke 18:35—24:53*, WBC 35c [Dallas: Word, 1993], 933–38; O'Toole, *Luke's Presentation of Jesus*, 50).

37. The same phrase appears in Deut. 32:35; Hos. 9:7.

cf. Jer. 25:9). Jerusalem's citizens "will fall by the edge of the sword [*stomata machairēs*]" just as they were struck down in the Babylonian invasion "by the edge of the sword [*stomata machairēs*]" (Luke 21:24; cf. Jer. 21:7).

These prophecies against Jerusalem—especially the temple sermon with its attendant prophetic action—lead to Jesus' arrest (Luke 19:47). The same is true of Jeremiah. Therefore, Luke adorns his account of Jesus' arrest with a few Jeremiah flourishes. Mark's story provides the template, while Jeremiah's story provides the distinctive vocabulary. According to Jeremiah's account, "Irijah would not listen [*ouk ēkousen*] to him, and seized [*synelaben*] Jeremiah and brought him to the rulers [*eisēgagon pros tous archontas*]. The rulers were embittered against Jeremiah and they beat him and sent him to the house [*eis tēn oikian*] of Jonathan, one of the scribes" (Jer. 37:14-15). None of this vocabulary describes the arrest of Mark's Jesus. "They laid hands on him and arrested [*ekratēsan*] him," says Mark. "They took [*apēgagon*] Jesus to the high priest" (Mark 14:46, 53). Luke, however, produces this sentence: "Then they seized [*syllabontes*] him and led him away, bringing him into the high priest's house [*eisēgagon eis tēn oikian tou archiereōs*]" (Luke 22:54). The arrest of Luke's Jesus is the arrest of a prophet like Jeremiah.[38]

What is more, the interrogation of Luke's Jesus is the interrogation of a prophet like Jeremiah. Luke emphasizes this by adding an interesting exchange to Mark's account of Jesus' trial before the Jerusalem council (Mark 14:55-60). "If you are the Messiah, tell us [*eipon hēmin*]," demand the chief priests, scribes, and elders. Jesus' response: "If I tell you, you will not believe; and if I question you, you will not answer [*ean hymin eipō, ou mē pisteusēte; ean de erōtēsō, ou mē apokrithēte*]" (Luke 22:66-68).

The vocabulary for this response seems to originate with an earlier interrogation by the chief priests, scribes, and elders—an interrogation recorded by Mark and reproduced by Luke. As Jesus teaches in the temple, these officials—who, according to Luke 19:47 were "looking for a way to kill him"—pose the following question: "Tell us [*eipon hēmin*], by what authority are you doing these things?" Jesus replies, "I will also ask you [*erōtēsō*] a question, and you tell me: Did the baptism of John come from heaven, or was it of

---

38. These echoes resound in Luke's account of John the Baptist's arrest. Here, too, Luke changes Mark's vocabulary. According to Mark, Herod's men "put him in prison [*edēsen auton en phylakē*]" (Mark 6:17). According to Luke, Herod added to his evil deeds "by shutting up [*katekleisen*] John in prison [*en phylakē*]" (Luke 3:20). The added verb seems to echo Jer. 32:2-3: "Jeremiah was imprisoned [*ephylasseto*] in the court of the guard [*phylakēs*] . . . in which King Zedekiah had shut [*katekleisen*] him up." Perhaps Luke sees John, too, as a prophet like Jeremiah.

human origin?" This puts Jesus' opponents in a quandary. If they agree that John's authority came from heaven, then Jesus will counter, "Why did you not believe [*ouk episteusate*] him?" On the other hand, they cannot claim that John's authority is merely human because the people will accuse them of blasphemy. "So they answered [*apekrithēsan*] that they did not know where it came from. Then Jesus said to them, 'Neither will I tell you [*legō hymin*] by what authority I am doing these things'" (Luke 20:1-8//Mark 11:27-33).

Luke changes Mark's version mostly by smoothing his syntax and deleting unnecessary words. He also makes a significant addition to the officials' initial question: "Tell us [*eipon hēmin*]" (Luke 20:2). He inserts the same clause into Mark's trial scene: "If you are the Messiah, tell us [*eipon hēmin*]" (Luke 22:67).[39] The repeated clause reinforces the verbal links between the two scenes. In the temple, Jesus "asks" the officials a straightforward question. Because they do not "believe," however, they cannot "answer." Therefore, Jesus will not "tell" them what they want to know—either in the temple or at his trial.[40]

The trial scene not only recapitulates the vocabulary of the temple controversy but also evokes one of Jeremiah's interrogations by King Zedekiah. Zedekiah says, "I will ask [*erōtēsō*] you something; do not hide anything from me." Jeremiah's response: "If I report anything to you, will you not put me to death? And if I advise you, you will not listen to me [*ean anangeilō soi, ouchi thanatō me thanatōseis; kai ean symbouleusō soi, ou mē akousēs mou*]" (Jer. 38:14-15).[41] The cadence, "If I . . . you will not; and if I . . . you will not . . . ," should seem familiar. Apparently, Jesus' response to the council in Luke 22:66-68 combines the vocabulary of Luke 20:1-8 with the structure of Jer. 38:14-15. This seems appropriate since all three scenes reflect similar circumstances. In each case, the Jerusalem authorities refuse to heed the prophet. Like Zedekiah, the chief priests, scribes, and elders continue on their predetermined course no matter what the prophet says. Therefore, like Jeremiah, Jesus refuses to engage with Jerusalem authorities who will not take him seriously.

The similarities between Jesus and Jeremiah end with this impasse. While Jeremiah goes on to survive the destruction of Solomon's temple, Jesus is executed before the Romans set fire to its replacement. Still, their respective judgment oracles come to pass. Because Jerusalem is not at peace with God,

---

39. Compare Luke 20:2; 22:67 to Mark 11:28; 14:61.

40. See also Tannehill, *Narrative Unity of Luke-Acts*, 1:190–91.

41. See also Neyrey, *The Passion According to Luke*, 73.

because God's people do not recognize the time of their visitation, the days of vengeance are upon them.

6

The Doom of Jerusalem

In the summer of 66 CE, the Roman governor of Judea appropriated a large sum from the temple treasury. This move sparked a rebellion that quickly spread from Jerusalem to Galilee. By the spring of 67, Vespasian was in Galilee with four Roman legions. It took him about a year to secure the region. In June of 68, he was advancing to Jerusalem when he received news of Nero's suicide. The ensuing chaos in Rome caused Vespasian to suspend operations in Judea. At the end of 69, Vespasian became emperor. Then, in the spring of 70, his son Titus pressed the siege of Jerusalem. The rebels held out for most of the summer, but by early September Titus ruled the city. There was not much left. More than one hundred thousand people had died during the siege; thousands more had been slaughtered once the city walls were breached.[1] Much of the destruction centered on the revolutionary headquarters: the temple and its adjoining fortress. The fortress was dismantled, and the temple, recently renovated by Herod the Great, was burned.

The loss of the temple struck a devastating blow to Jews everywhere. With it went a major economic center and source of national pride. With it went the daily sacrifice, the solemn festival observances, and the performance of personal rites. With it went the visible symbol of God's presence. And with it went first-century hopes for redemption by a messiah who would defeat the Romans and restore Jerusalem to its former glory. The revolution, fueled by such hopes, had ended in bitter disappointment.[2]

The loss of the temple was devastating not only for Jews but also for Christians. Some Christians may have been tempted to believe that one of

1. Josephus puts the total at 1.1 million dead with 97,000 captured over the course of the conflict (*J.W.* 6.420).

2. That the Jewish War was fueled by messianic hopes is supported by coinage that features grapevines, a motif derived from prophecies that associate the advent of the messiah with an abundance of wine (Amos 9:11, 13-14; *2 Bar.* 29:3, 5-6). See Ya'akov Meshorer, *Jewish Coins of the Second Temple Period* (Tel Aviv: Am Hassefer, 1967), 164–69, plates 19–28. Messianic hopes would be revived in the Bar Kokhba revolt of 132–136.

the revolutionary leaders was the Messiah.[3] At least two of those leaders seem to have made royal claims.[4] Surely the revolt presented the best opportunity for God's anointed king to fulfill prophecies of victory over the Gentiles and restoration for Jerusalem and the temple. Now, with Jerusalem laid waste and the temple in ruins, all bets were off. Restoration had become much more difficult to imagine.[5]

Luke deals with the loss of the temple in much the same way that he addresses concerns about a crucified messiah, Gentile inclusion, and Jewish rejection. He assures his audience that this, too, was part of God's plan. Accordingly, Luke's Jesus foresees the doom of Jerusalem and prophesies it numerous times. In his woes, parables, and judgment oracles, he accuses the temple authorities of abusing God's trust and opposing God's Messiah. The sentence: God will destroy them together with the temple.[6]

Since it might seem strange—especially in the messianic age—that God should move against God's own sanctuary, Luke reminds his audience of the precedent set by Israel's prophets. Luke's Jesus uses their language to condemn Jerusalem and describe its doom. Jeremiah, who prophesied the destruction of the first temple, is the most obvious source for such language. Luke therefore cites Jeremiah along with other prophets who speak of siege and slaughter, captivity and destruction. For Luke, the Jesus who utters woes, parables, and judgment oracles against Jerusalem is a prophet like Hosea, Zephaniah, Zechariah, Isaiah, Jeremiah, Isaiah, and Ezekiel. In their day, God sent Gentile armies against his people. Now, after the first coming of the Messiah, God will send them again, for many of the same reasons.[7]

"As a Fulfillment of All That Is Written"

As Luke and his associates tried to process the significance of the war and its aftermath, they turned to the Scriptures. Descriptions of cities under attack now resonated with grim undertones. The hordes of armed invaders; their siege towers and battering rams; the dreaded moment when the wall was breached and the slaughter began; the rotting corpses; the naked prisoners; the ruined city and its ravaged countryside: all this and more haunted their imaginations.

---

3. Mark 13:6, 21-22 reflects an apparent attempt to dissuade them.

4. Josephus, *J.W.* 4.390, 510.

5. David L. Tiede emphasizes the importance of this issue for Luke (*Prophecy and History in Luke-Acts* [Philadelphia: Fortress Press, 1980], 1–7, 120).

6. Donald Juel, *Luke-Acts: The Promise of History* (Atlanta: John Knox, 1983), 48–49.

7. According to C. H. Dodd, "The prototype for the coming disaster is the Babylonian capture of Jerusalem in 586 B.C." ("The Fall of Jerusalem and the 'Abomination of Desolation,'" *JRS* 37 [1947]: 53).

The ancient stories had become their story. The laments spoke their anguish, and the prophecies seemed to reflect Roman as well as Assyrian and Babylonian invasion.

Many of those prophecies portray God as the invader. God plans the siege; God wields the sword; God binds the captives in chains. According to Isaiah, God sends the Assyrians against Jerusalem:

> And like David I will surround you [epi se]
>> and lay a rampart [kai balō peri se charaka] around you and
> place towers around you. (Isa. 29:3)

Zephaniah describes the day of the Lord:

> The great [megalē] day of the Lord is near,
>> near and hastening quickly. . . .
> That day will be a day of wrath [orgēs],
>> a day of tribulation and distress [anagkēs]. (Zeph. 1:14-15)

For Ezekiel and Jeremiah, the Babylonians become the God's agents of slaughter. Ezekiel receives instructions for making a model of Jerusalem under siege:

> Lay a rampart around it [peribaleis ep' autēn charaka]. (Ezek 4:2)

Jeremiah envisions the attack:

> Look, I will send and take hold of the people from the north, and I will bring them against this land [epi tēn gēn] and against its inhabitants and against all the nations around it. I will make them desolate [exerēmōsō]; I will make them an example of destruction, an object of hissing, and an everlasting disgrace. (Jer. 25:9)

> And after these things, says the Lord, I will give King Zedekiah of Judah and his servants and the people in this city—the people left by death and hunger and the sword—into the hands of their enemies [echthrōn] who seek their lives. They will cut them down with the edge of the sword [stomata machairas]. I will not spare them, and I will not by any means have compassion on them. (Jer. 21:7)

> That day is for the Lord our God

> a day of vengeance [*hēmera ekdikēseōs*],
> to take vengeance on his enemies.
> The sword of the Lord will devour and be satisfied
> and get drunk on their blood. (Jer. 46:10)

Other prophets join the chorus. Hosea depicts ruthless infanticide; Ezekiel describes captivity and exile:

> Destruction will rise up among your people
> and all your walls will be ruined.
> As Salaman, ruler from the house of Jerubbaal, in the days of battle
> crushed a mother with her children [*mētera epi teknois ēdaphisan*],
> so will I do to you, O house of Israel. (Hos. 10:14-15)
> I will provoke to anger the heart of many peoples
> when I bring your captives [*aichmalōsian*] among the nations [*eis ta ethnē*]
> into a land that you do not know. (Ezek. 32:9)[8]

The invaded city becomes a desolate, disgraceful ruin:

> I forsook my house [*ton oikon mou*];
> I abandoned [*aphēka*] my heritage;
> I gave my beloved soul
> into the hands of its enemies. (Jer. 12:7)

And I took the cup from the Lord's hand and made the nations to whom the Lord sent me drink it: Jerusalem and the cities of Judah . . . to make them a desolation [*erēmōsin*] and a waste and an object of hissing. (Jer. 25:17-18; cf. 44:6, 22)

Look, I am placing Jerusalem as a tottering front porch among all the surrounding people, and in Judea there will be a siege against

---

8. Hosea 10:14-15 refers to an invasion of Samaria; Ezek. 32:9, to an invasion of Egypt.

Jerusalem. On that day I will make Jerusalem a stone trampled by all the nations [*Ierousalēm lithon katapatoumenon pasin tois ethnesin*]. Everyone who tramples it will mock it, and all the nations of the earth will gather together against it. (Zech. 12:2-3)

> Thistles and thorns will grow up on their sacrificial altars.
> They will say to the mountains [*erousin tois oresin*], "Cover us [*kalypsate hēmas*]"
>> and to the hills [*kai tois bounois*], "Fall on us [*pesate eph' hēmas*]!" (Hos. 10:8)

It is painful enough simply to read these passages, so sharply do they delineate the destruction of a beloved city and the murder of its people. When that city is the reader's city and its people the reader's people, however, the pain becomes unbearable. We can only imagine the anguish of the many Christians for whom this was the case. They could now empathize fully with Jeremiah, the prophet who so openly expresses his emotions:

> Who will give water for my head
>> and a fountain of tears for my eyes?
> And I will weep [*klausomai*] for this people, my people;
>> day and night for the wounded of the daughter of my people. (Jer. 9:1)

No doubt some of them did weep day and night until there were no tears left.

Their anguish raised an important question. If God planned the siege, wielded the sword, and bound the captives, why did God do it? If the invasion marks God's "day of vengeance," for what is vengeance required? Once more, a search of Jeremiah's prophecies turns up some answers:

> They tried to heal the fracture of my people with contempt,
>> saying, "Peace, peace [*eirēnē eirēnē*],"
>> and where is peace [*eirēnē*]? . . .
> Therefore they will collapse in their falling,
>> and in the time of their visitation [*en kairō episkopēs*] they will perish, says the Lord. (Jer. 6:14-15)

> There are no grapes on the vines;

> there are no figs on the fig trees [*sykais*];
> even the leaves have fallen off. . . .
> God has cast us out
> and has given us water with gall to drink
> because we sinned before him.
> (Jer. 8:13-14)

Unless they turn back [*ean de mē epistrepsōsin*], I will remove that nation with destruction and annihilation [*apōleia*]. (Jer. 12:17)

In Jeremiah's day, God destroyed Jerusalem because of the people's willful ignorance and refusal to repent. In Luke's day, it must have seemed logical to conclude that God was doing the same.

"JERUSALEM, JERUSALEM"

Luke has access to these prophecies—prophecies that describe a terrible invasion, mourn the devastation, and explain its cause. As he crafts Jesus' oracles against Jerusalem and the temple, he appropriates some of their vocabulary. In addition, he incorporates Jeremiah-like sayings from Q and Mark. The result is a string of laments and judgment oracles, illustrated with parables and prophetic actions, in which Jesus prophesies the Jewish War using the language of Hosea, Zephaniah, Zechariah, Isaiah, Jeremiah, and Ezekiel.

Luke's Jesus begins to prophesy against Jerusalem on his journey to the Holy City. He starts with three sayings borrowed from Q. The first is the pronouncement of woe to Pharisees and lawyers whose ancestors murdered the prophets (Luke 11:47-51//Matt. 23:29-36). As we have seen, Jesus accuses them of witnessing and approving the deeds of their ancestors. We have also noted Jesus' warning with its allusions to Jeremiah and 2 Chronicles:

From the day that their ancestors came out of the land of Egypt even until this day, I sent to you [*exapesteila pros hymas*] all my servants the prophets [*prophētas*]. I sent them day after day but they did not listen [*ouk ēkousan*] to me; they did not incline their ear and they stiffened their necks even more than their ancestors did. (Jer. 7:25-26)

And although I sent to you [*apestellon pros hymas*] my servants the prophets [*prophētas*] early in the morning, you neither listened [*ouk eisēkousate*] nor inclined your ear. (Jer. 25:4)

He sent to them prophets [*apesteilen pros autous prophētas*] to turn them to the Lord but they did not listen [*ouk ēkousan*]. They warned them but they did not listen [*ouk ēkousan*]. (2 Chron. 24:19)

Therefore the Wisdom of God said, "I will send them prophets and apostles [*apostelō eis autous prophētas kai apostolous*], some of whom they will kill and persecute." (Luke 11:49)

Jesus' warning implicates the Pharisees and lawyers in the murder of all God's prophets, ancient and contemporary.

Jesus does not stop there, however. He goes on to cite Abel and Zechariah, two biblical murder victims who cry for vengeance (Luke 11:51//Matt. 23:35). Abel, a son of Adam and Eve, unwittingly provoked his brother Cain to jealousy. When Cain killed Abel, Abel's blood cried out to God from the ground (Gen. 4:1-16). Zechariah's story, set in the court of King Joash of Jerusalem (837–800 BCE), follows the indictment in 2 Chron. 24:19, which says that the Lord sent prophets but that the people did not listen. Zechariah was one such prophet. "Because you have forsaken the Lord, he will also forsake you," he said (2 Chron. 24:20). The people, however, objected to Zechariah's warning. "They set upon him and, on King Joash's orders, stoned [*elithobolēsan*] him in the court of the house of the Lord. . . . As he was dying, he said, 'May the Lord see and judge!'" (2 Chron. 24:22).

Abel and Zechariah form a kind of historical synechdoche. The former is killed at the beginning of Genesis; the latter, near the end of 2 Chronicles. Together they represent all the prophets murdered by the Pharisees' and lawyers' ancestors—prophets whose murders have yet to be avenged. Jesus warns the Pharisees and lawyers that, when they kill Jesus and his followers, they will not only assume responsibility for the murders of all the prophets but also suffer the consequences. "Yes, I tell you, it shall be required of this generation" (Luke 11:51//Matt 23:36).

It is not at all clear from this woe that God's retribution will include the Jewish War and the destruction of the temple. The next two prophecies, however, indicate that this is just what Luke has in mind. Recall that Luke's Jesus introduces the Q lament over Jerusalem by explaining that he is on his way to Jerusalem because a prophet cannot be killed anywhere else (Luke 13:33). The lament itself begins like this: "Jerusalem, Jerusalem, the city that kills the prophets [*tous prophētas*] and stones [*lithobolousa*] those who are sent [*apestalmenous*] to it!" (Luke 13:34//Matt. 23:37). It echoes the woe to Pharisees and lawyers with its embedded story of Zechariah, stoned to death in the temple. It also includes this cryptic statement: "Your house is left to you [*aphietai hymin ho oikos hymōn*]" (Luke 13:35//Matt. 23:38). According to Jer. 12:7, this expression refers to the temple. The Q lament with its Lukan introduction thus seems to work like a judgment oracle. The accusation: Jerusalem kills the prophets, including Jesus. The sentence: God will forsake Jerusalem's temple.

Luke's Jesus illustrates his oracles with the parable of the Ten Pounds (Luke 19:11-27). A version of this parable also appears in Matthew (Matt. 25:14-30). There is some debate as to whether it belongs to Q. There are significant differences in vocabulary and detail. Still, the two versions share the same basic story line. The most important sayings—the rebuke of the wicked slave and the final aphorism—are remarkably similar. In my view, a Q origin is highly possible. Still, whether the basic tradition originated with Q or some other source, a parable about the important subject of judgment would have warranted extensive editing by both Matthew and Luke. Since each evangelist pursued his own distinctive agenda on the topic, the results would have appeared much like the extant parables: one version (Matthew's) that emphasizes high stakes, great rewards, and severe punishments; another (Luke's) that depicts a coming kingdom with retribution not only for the king's negligent slaves but also for his enemies.

For our purposes, the important point is how Luke's version illustrates his characteristic portrayal of Jesus and his opponents. First, Luke explains that Jesus tells the parable because proximity to Jerusalem puts the coming messianic kingdom on his followers' minds. The parable indicates that what happens to Jesus there will defy all their expectations. The nobleman represents Jesus, an unusual kind of messiah. Instead of ascending to a throne in Jerusalem, he ascends into heaven, where God gives him royal power.[9] His enemies are not Gentiles but "the citizens of his country" (Luke 19:14). The parable directly links their opposition to a grisly fate: "As for those enemies of mine who did not want me to be king over them—bring them here and slaughter them in my presence!" (Luke 19:27). This messianic kingdom spells disaster for Jews who reject Jesus' rule.

In the wake of these two judgment oracles and one prophetic parable, Luke clarifies the accusation and sentence in a second lament over Jerusalem (Luke 19:41-44). This lament, found only in Luke, ends Jesus' journey. It resonates with echoes of words, phrases, and situations from Isaiah and Hosea, bracketed by two accusations from one of Jeremiah's judgment oracles. As we have seen,

---

9. Cf. Luke 24:51; Acts 1:9; 2:34-36.

Luke introduces the lament with an implicit comparison to that prophet: "As [Jesus] came near and saw the city, he wept [*eklausen*] over it" (Luke 19:41; cf. Jer. 9:1). Jesus goes on to explain his outburst: as in the days of Jeremiah, its inhabitants do not recognize "the things that make for peace [*ta pros eirēnēn*]" (Luke 19:42; cf. Jer. 6:14).

He follows this accusation with a detailed sentence. A description of the coming siege echoes Isaiah and Ezekiel: "Indeed, the days will come upon you [*epi se*], when your enemies will set up ramparts around you [*kai parembalousin hoi echthroi sou charaka soi*] and surround you, and hem you in on every side" (Luke 19:43; cf. Isa. 29:3; Ezek. 4:2).[10] Hosea lends the vocabulary to describe the terrors in store: "They will crush you and your children within you [*edaphiousin se kai ta tekna sou en soi*]" (Luke 19:44; cf. Hos. 10:14).[11] Jesus ends with a second accusation from Jeremiah: "You did not recognize the time of your visitation [*ton kairon tēs episkopēs sou*] from God" (Luke 19:44; cf. Jer. 6:15).[12] This is Luke's most explicit explanation for the destruction of Jerusalem: it results from Jewish rejection of Jesus, God's prophet and God's Messiah.

"DAYS OF VENGEANCE"

As Jesus journeys to Jerusalem, Luke builds the expectation of his arrival. Brief notices that he is "on the way" lead to a sudden crescendo of milestones near the journey's end. Jesus is "going up to Jerusalem"; he enters Jericho; he draws near to Jerusalem; he has reached the Mount of Olives; he sees the city.[13] The crescendo builds in the lament of Luke 19:41-44 and reaches a climax in Luke 19:45: "Then he entered the temple."

His first deed there is a prophetic action. Driving out the merchants illustrates an accusation borrowed from Mark's quotation of Isaiah and Jeremiah:

It is written,
"My house shall be a house of prayer";
   but you have made it a den of robbers. (Luke 19:46//Mark 11:17)

10. Dodd, "Fall of Jerusalem," 50; Luke Timothy Johnson, *The Gospel of Luke*, SP 3 (Collegeville, MN: Liturgical, 1991), 299; David L. Tiede, *Prophecy and History in Luke-Acts*, 82n22; Joel B. Green, *The Gospel of Luke*, NICNT (Grand Rapids: Eerdmans, 1997), 691n38.

11. Dodd, "Fall of Jerusalem"; Jerome Neyrey, *The Passion According to Luke: A Redaction Study of Luke's Soteriology* (New York: Paulist, 1985), 116; Johnson, *Gospel of Luke*, 299.

12. Dodd, "Fall of Jerusalem," 51.

13. Luke 13:22; 17:11; 18:31, 35; 19:1, 11, 28, 29, 37, 41.

We have already observed that the accusation conflates two prophecies about God's house:

> My house will be called a house of prayer
> for all the nations. (Isa. 56:7)

> My house—there, where my name is invoked on it—has not become
> a den of robbers, has it? (Jer. 7:11)

Mark, who sandwiches this scene between Jesus' cursing a barren fig tree and the tree's withering to its roots, uses the entire unit to foreshadow the events of 70 CE (Mark 11:12-21). For Mark, as well as for Luke, the temple was asking to be withered to its roots. It was not a house where people assembled to raise their prayers, producing fruit for God. It was a barren house where profiteers assembled to divide the spoils.

Although Luke agrees with the force of Mark's indictment, he omits the two fig tree scenes. Like Mark, however, he follows the prophetic action with a prophetic parable: the parable of the Wicked Tenants (Luke 20:9-19//Mark 12:1-12).[14] Its story of miserly tenant-farmers illustrates the accusation from Isaiah and Jeremiah with a transparent critique of the temple authorities, interested more in profits than in prayers. It also levels a second, more serious accusation: the temple authorities abuse God's servants and kill God's Son. At this point, the parable presents its typical call for judgment along with a terrible sentence: "What then will the owner of the vineyard do? He will come and destroy those tenants and give the vineyard to others" (Luke 20:16). Jesus illustrates the sentence by quoting Ps. 118:22:

> The stone that the builders rejected
> has become the cornerstone. (Luke 20:17)

Luke is not the first to link Jewish rejection of Jesus with the end of the temple cult. He simply elaborates a connection already present in Mark.

This elaboration comes to the fore in response to exclamations "about the temple, how it was adorned with beautiful stones and gifts dedicated to God" (Luke 21:5//Mark 13:1). For Luke, as for Mark, admiration of the temple cues Jesus' apocalyptic discourse. Mark's version includes a cryptic description of the Roman siege—a description that Luke extensively edits (Luke 21:20-24//Mark 13:14-20). By inserting phrases from Jeremiah, Ezekiel, and Zechariah, Luke

---

14. Luke removes any possible allusions to Isa. 5:1-7 from Mark's parable.

portrays Jesus as a prophet who foretells the coming horrors in more explicit terms, portraying them "as a fulfillment of all that is written" (Luke 21:22). When armies surround Jerusalem, there will be "desolation [*erēmōsis*]" and "days of vengeance [*hēmerai ekdikēseōs*]" as in the time of Jeremiah (Luke 21:20, 22; cf. Jer. 25:18; 44:6, 22; 46:10).[15] Jesus describes the ensuing slaughter, captivity, and degradation using phrases from Jeremiah, Ezekiel, Zephaniah, and Zechariah: "There will be great distress on the [land] and wrath [*anagkē megalē epi tēs gēs kai orgē*] against this people; they will fall by the edge of the sword [*stomata machairēs*] and be taken away as captives among all nations [*aichmalōtisthēsontai eis ta ethnē panta*]; and Jerusalem will be trampled on by the Gentiles [*Ierousalēm estai patoumenē hypo ethnōn*]" (Luke 21:23-24; cf. Jer. 25:9; 21:7; Ezek. 32:9; Zeph. 1:14-15; Zech. 12:3).[16]

Even on the way to his execution, Luke's Jesus continues to foretell the siege. In a scene that appears only in Luke, women of Jerusalem lament the condemned Messiah. "Daughters of Jerusalem," replies Jesus, "do not weep for me, but weep for yourselves and for your children" (Luke 23:27-28). Because he is a prophet, Jesus knows what is in store for them. "The days are surely coming," he says, "when they will say, 'Blessed are the barren, and the wombs that never bore, and the breasts that never nursed'" (Luke 23:9).[17] Jesus follows this warning by quoting Hos. 10:8: "They will begin to say to the mountains [*legein tois oresin*], 'Fall on us [*pesete eph' hēmas*]'; and to the hills [*kai tois bounois*], 'Cover us [*kalypsate hēmas*]'"(Luke 23:29).[18] He ends the oracle with a question: "If they do this when the wood is green, what will happen when it is dry?" (Luke 23:30-31). For the last time, Jesus makes an implicit connection between his execution and the fate of Jerusalem. If the Romans murder the Messiah, surely they will not hesitate to annihilate the Holy City.

"Unless You Repent"

Was it inevitable that Galilee should be ravaged and the temple destroyed? When Jerusalem kills the prophet Jesus, does that seal the city's fate? Luke's

15. Cf. also Deut. 32:35; Hos. 9:7. Dodd, "Fall of Jerusalem," 49, 51; Neyrey, *The Passion According to Luke*, 117–18.

16. Dodd, "Fall of Jerusalem," 51–52; Tiede, *Prophecy and History in Luke-Acts*, 92; Neyrey, *The Passion According to Luke*, 118; C. F. Evans, *Saint Luke*, TPINTC (London: SCM, 1990), 751; Green, *Gospel of Luke*, 739n40.

17. Luke may base the saying on Mark 13:17//Luke 21:23: "Woe to those who are pregnant and to those who are nursing infants in those days!"

18. Neyrey, *The Passion According to Luke*, 113. The quotation is only slightly altered.

Jesus seems certain about the coming siege and consequent slaughter—but he also hints that they can avoid their doom. This is possible because, in Luke's view, untimely death is a punishment for sin. The Galileans killed by Pilate; the Jerusalemites crushed by a falling tower: they were sinners (Luke 13:1-5). Everyone else in Galilee and Jerusalem is just as bad, if not worse. Therefore, Jesus issues his Jeremiah-like warning: "Unless you repent [ean mē metanoēte], you will all perish [apoleisthe] as they did" (Luke 13:3, 5; cf. Jer. 12:17). What if they do repent? In that case, one presumes, they might not perish.

We have noticed that Jesus illustrates this call to repentance with the parable of the Barren Fig Tree (Luke 13:6-9). It seems to replace the fig tree scenes of Mark 11:12-21. Instead of cursing a fig tree so that it withers to its roots, Luke's Jesus tells a story about a fig tree (sykē) that is not immediately destroyed. The tree grows in a vineyard whose owner expects it to bear fruit. As in the parable of the Wicked Tenants (Luke 20:9-19//Mark 11:1-12), the vineyard represents Jerusalem; the owner, God. The barren fig tree parable mentions no tenants, however. It does not even mention produce. It concerns one fig tree that for three years has not borne fruit. As in Jeremiah's oracle, "There are no figs on the fig trees [sykais]; . . . because we have sinned before him" (Jer. 8:13). "Cut it down [ekkopson autēn]!" the owner tells his gardener. "Why should it be wasting the soil?" (Luke 13:7).

The gardener, however, intercedes for the tree: "Let it alone for one more year, until I dig around it and put manure on it. If it bears fruit [poiēsē karpon] next year, well and good; but if not, you can cut it down [ekkopseis autēn]"(Luke 13:8-9). The language of "bearing fruit" and "cutting down" evokes Q's warnings as delivered by John the Baptist: "Bear fruits [poiēsate oun karpous] worthy of repentance. . . . Every tree therefore that does not bear good fruit [poioun karpon kalon] is cut down [ekkoptetai] and thrown into the fire" (Luke 3:8-9//Matt. 3:8-10).[19] Luke's parable gives Jerusalem an opportunity to repent and bear fruit. With a little more tending—this time from Jesus' apostles—the people might yet avoid their fate.[20]

---

19. See also Robert C. Tannehill, *The Narrative Unity of Luke-Acts: A Literary Interpretation* (Philadelphia: Fortress Press, 1986), 1:50–51.

20. See also Johnson, *Gospel of Luke*, 214.

7

Prophets Like Jesus

The Acts of the Apostles begins with a flashback to the ending of Luke's Gospel. The apostles are in Jerusalem. The Messiah had been executed, but God has raised him from the dead. Naturally, the apostles wonder what will happen next. "Lord," they ask, "is it at this time when you will restore the kingdom to Israel?" (Acts 1:6). Perhaps now Jesus will defeat the Romans who crucified him. Perhaps now God will set God's king on Zion, empowering him to "break them with a rod of iron" and "dash them in pieces like a potter's vessel."

God, however, has another plan. Jesus tells the apostles, "It is not for you to know the times or periods that the Father has set by his own authority" (Acts 1:7).[1] God might restore the kingdom now or God might wait—how long, nobody knows. Meanwhile, the apostles must play an important role. Jesus explains it in his last words to them: "You will receive power when the Holy Spirit has come upon you, and you will be my witnesses in Jerusalem, in all Judea and Samaria, and to the ends of the earth" (Acts 1:8). Now that the apostles have seen the risen Jesus, now that he has "presented himself alive to them by many convincing proofs" (Acts 1:3), they will testify to the good news of Jesus the Messiah among Jews, Samaritans, and Gentiles.

Jesus' commission in Acts 1:8 sets up the book's plot. The story begins in Jerusalem, where the apostles—chiefly Peter and John, along with the *diakonos* Stephen—proclaim the good news (Acts 2:14—8:3).[2] When Stephen is stoned to death, the apostles flee Jerusalem. In Samaria, the *diakonos* Philip and the

---

1. Luke borrows this statement from his sources. Cf. Mark 13:32; Matt 24:44//Luke 12:40.

2. When Luke's characters witness the resurrection and then testify to others, Luke consistently involves at least two men (Luke 24:4-7, 13-53; Acts 1:1-11; 3:1—4:22; 5:12-42; 8:14-25; 10:23-48; 11:12; 13:2—14:28; 15:40—17:15; 18:18-28). He carefully adheres to Moses' standard for valid testimony: "the evidence of two or three witnesses" (Num. 35:30; Deut. 17:6; 19:15). Exceptions include Philip's preaching in Samaria (Acts 8:4-13), his preaching on the Gaza road (vv. 26-40), Paul's testimony in Athens (17:22-31), and Paul's speeches in his defense (e.g., Acts 23:1-6; 24:10-21; 26:1-29). In the first three cases, Philip and Paul testify outside Judea; at Paul's trials, he does not present evidence but rather rebuts the testimony of others.

apostles Peter and John preach in the city and among the towns and villages (Acts 8:4-25). The good news also begins to reach people from the ends of the earth: an Ethiopian eunuch in Acts 8:26-40; a Roman centurion in Acts 10:1-48. The major transition, however, comes in Acts 11:19, where Luke reports that Stephen's death scattered believers "as far as Phoenicia, Cyprus, and Antioch." Paul and his companions will now bring the good news from Antioch to Asia Minor, Macedonia, Achaia, Crete, and Rome (Acts 11:19—28:31).

Peter and Paul are the most prominent apostles. As Luke describes their testimony to Jesus' resurrection, he portrays them as prophets. Unlike John the Baptist and Jesus, however, they are not prophets from birth. They are commissioned by Jesus in scenes that resemble prophetic call narratives and then launched on prophetic careers like his.[3] Filled with the Holy Spirit, they confront evil powers and preach sermons. They perform miracles, see visions, know people's thoughts, and utter judgment oracles. They are arrested and tried before the Jerusalem council. Many of these parallels extend to the *diakonoi* Stephen and Philip. They, too, are filled with the Holy Spirit. They, too, perform miracles. Like Jesus, Stephen prophesies against the temple. Like Jesus, he is rejected by the council in Jerusalem and executed there.

Peter and Paul resemble Jesus in two other important ways. Because Jesus is a prophet like Elijah, his followers Peter and Paul become prophets like Elisha. Peter sees Jesus ascend into heaven. Peter and Paul receive Jesus' spirit and perform his miracles, even when the beneficiaries are Gentiles. In addition, Peter and Paul continue in the prophetic tradition of Moses. They receive Jesus' spirit; they perform signs and wonders. When their own people reject them as they rejected Jesus, it therefore comes as no surprise. Moses, too, was rejected twice: once by the Hebrew whom he tried to save and once by the Israelites who turned their back on God to worship an idol. By portraying Peter and Paul as prophets like Elisha and Moses, Luke effectively legitimates Gentile inclusion and Jewish rejection. Once more, the prophets set the precedent.

"Catching People"

Luke devotes about one-third of Acts to Peter's career. Peter leads the believing community from the very beginning (Acts 1:15). Filled with the Holy Spirit, he preaches the good news about God's offer of salvation (Acts 2:14-41; 3:11-26; 4:8-12, 31; 10:34-43). His converts include thousands of Jews, many Samaritans, and a household of Romans (Acts 2:41; 4:4; 5:14; 8:25; 10:44-48). He heals two

---

3. Luke Timothy Johnson, *The Literary Function of Possessions in Luke-Acts*, SBLDS 39 (Missoula, MT: Scholars Press, 1977), 60.

paralytics and raises a dead woman (Acts 3:1-10; 9:32-43). His reputation drives sick people to line the streets, hoping for his shadow to fall on them (Acts 5:15). Other apostles display similar powers (Acts 2:43; 3:4; 4:1; 5:12, 16, 42).

These are not the disciples we know from Mark's Gospel: disciples who, after participating in two miraculous feedings, worry when they have only one loaf; disciples who cannot believe that the Messiah will be killed; disciples who request the places of honor on either side of his royal throne; disciples who, when Jesus asks them to pray, fall asleep three times; disciples who promise never to desert him only to deny any knowledge of him (Mark 8:14-21, 27-33; 10:35-40; 14:29-42, 66-72). Because Luke realizes this, he makes a few changes to Mark's account. He omits the embarrassing episodes of the one loaf and the request for places of honor. Other scenes are too important to omit, so Luke alters them. When Luke's Jesus predicts his passion, Peter does not rebuke Jesus, nor does Jesus chastise Peter (Luke 9:18-22). At Gethsemane, Peter, James, and John fall asleep only once, because of grief; in the high priest's courtyard, Peter denies Jesus under temporary pressure from Satan (Luke 22:31-32, 39-46). Luke makes these changes because his story, unlike Mark's, continues in Volume 2. Luke's Peter and his companions will receive the Holy Spirit, perform miracles, and speak the word of God with boldness. They cannot look like fools in Volume 1.

Instead, they must look like future prophets. Therefore, in addition to erasing traces of foolish behavior, Luke adds details that set up Peter and his companions for prophetic careers. He begins at the earliest possible opportunity with the account of Jesus calling his first disciples. Mark tells the story in a few brief sentences. Jesus is walking by the Sea of Galilee when he spots four fishermen: Peter, Andrew, James, and John. He offers to make them fishers for people, and they follow him (Mark 1:16-20). Strangely, Mark never explains how Jesus convinced them to leave their livelihoods. He just describes how they did it: "immediately."

Luke fills in the missing details (Luke 5:1-11). He transforms the scene into a prophetic call narrative—an episode that starts a prophet's career with God's manifestation, God's commission, and God's enabling.[4] Why does Luke's Peter follow Jesus? He follows because Jesus has just orchestrated a huge haul of fish. The miraculous catch is as much a manifestation of God's power and presence in Jesus as, for example, Isaiah's vision of the divine king in the temple (Isa. 6:1-4). What is more, both theophanies elicit a strong sense of inadequacy from the prophet-to-be. In response, God not only charges the prophet with his task but also makes him competent to perform it. In Isaiah's case, unclean lips

---

4. See Exod. 3:1—4:17; 1 Sam. 3:1-14; Isa. 6:1-13; Jer. 1:4-10; Ezek. 1:1—3:27.

prevent him from speaking God's word. The Lord must purify Isaiah's lips and cleanse his sins before telling him, "Go and [speak] to this people" (Isa. 6:5-9). Similarly, Peter falls down, saying, "Go away from me, Lord, for I am a sinful man!" Jesus then tells him, "Do not be afraid; from now on you will be catching people" (Luke 5:8-10). No wonder Peter and his companions leave everything to follow Jesus.[5]

"THEY SHALL PROPHESY"

Peter does not haul in a large catch of people until the beginning of Acts. This is because God does not enable Peter until after Jesus' crucifixion, resurrection, and ascension. Only then is Peter filled with the Holy Spirit. Only then does he preach a sermon about the Messiah with the result that "about three thousand persons were added" (Acts 2:41). Only then does he become a prophet like Jesus. Because it is so important for Luke to show that God has transferred Jesus' prophetic ministry to Peter and the apostles, he carefully constructs the scenario. The Spirit that they receive is the same Spirit that Jesus surrendered at his death. It falls on them after their teacher has ascended into heaven. Then, empowered by his Spirit, they perform his works. In sum, the transfer of Jesus' Spirit to the apostles resembles the transfer of Elijah's spirit to Elisha.[6] Just as Elisha becomes a prophet like Elijah, so the apostles become prophets like Jesus.

The Elijah-Elisha transfer takes place in 2 Kgs. 2:1-12. The Lord is "about to bring Elijah up into heaven [*eis ton ouranon*] by a whirlwind" (2 Kgs. 2:1). Elijah asks his disciple Elisha, "Ask what I may do for you, before I am taken up from you [*analēmphthē . . . apo sou*]?" "All right, then," says Elisha. "Let there be a double share of your spirit [*pneumati*] upon me" (2 Kgs. 2:9). Elijah replies, "If you see me as I am being taken up from you [*ean idēs me analambanomenon apo sou*], it will be so for you" (2 Kgs. 2:10). Then, as Elijah and Elisha walk and talk together, fiery chariots and horses separate them. Elijah is taken up (*analēmphthē*)

---

5. See also Luke Timothy Johnson, *The Gospel of Luke*, SP 3 (Collegeville, MN: Liturgical, 1991), 33; Joel B. Green, *The Gospel of Luke*, NICNT (Grand Rapids: Eerdmans, 1997), 232. Luke may have styled this scene after Isaiah's call narrative. He certainly reflected a great deal on Isaiah's commission (cf. Isa. 6:9-10 in Luke 8:10; Acts 28:26-27).

6. P. Dabeck, "Siehe, es erschienen Moses und Elias," *Bib* 23 (1942): 183; G. W. H. Lampe, "The Holy Spirit in the Writings of St Luke," in *Studies in the Gospels*, ed. D. E. Nineham (Oxford: Blackwell, 1955), 177; Lampe, "The Lucan Portrait of Christ," *NTS* 2 (1955–1956): 169; Paul Hinnebusch, "Jesus, the New Elijah, in Saint Luke," *TBT* 32 (1967): 2241; Jean-Daniel Dubois, "La Figure d'Elie dans la Perspective Lucanienne," *RHPR* 53 (1973): 170; Richard I. Pervo, *Acts: A Commentary*, Hermeneia (Minneapolis: Fortress Press, 2008), 45–46.

by a whirlwind into heaven (*eis ton ouranon*). Meanwhile, Elisha keeps watching (*heōra*) until he can no longer see (*eidon*; 2 Kings 2:11-12).

Elisha has fulfilled the qualifications for receiving a double share of Elijah's spirit. Therefore, God grants his request. His fellow prophets recognize this right away. "The spirit [*pneuma*] of Elijah rests on Elisha," they say (2 Kgs. 2:15). Elisha then begins to perform some of Elijah's signature miracles. He parts the Jordan River, controls the water supply, and multiplies the oil in a woman's jar (2 Kgs. 2:14; 3:13-20; 4:1-7).[7] He stays with a patroness in an "upper room [*hyperōon*]" where he raises the woman's dead son (2 Kgs. 4:8-37).[8] Clearly, Elisha has inherited the prophetic spirit of his teacher Elijah.

How then does Luke show that the apostles inherit the prophetic spirit of their teacher Jesus? First, he portrays Jesus as a spirit-filled prophet, adding the necessary descriptions to Mark's story. After Jesus is baptized (*baptisthēnai*), "the Holy Spirit [*to pneuma to hagion*]" descends on him (Luke 3:22//Mark 1:10). "Full of the Holy Spirit [*plērēs pneumatos hagiou*]," Jesus sojourns in the wilderness (Luke 4:1). In "the power of the Spirit [*pneumatos*]," he returns to Galilee (Luke 4:14). At the synagogue in Nazareth, he preaches his inaugural sermon. His text is a prophecy about the Holy Spirit, now being fulfilled: "The Spirit [*pneuma*] of the Lord is upon me" (Luke 4:18; cf. Isa 61:1).

Next, Luke's Jesus begins to perform some signature miracles. One of the first involves the paralytic let down through the roof. After suggesting that it would be difficult to say, "Rise and walk [*egeire kai peripatei*]," Jesus tells the man, "Stand up [*egeire*] and take your bed and go to your home" (Luke 5:23-24//Mark 2:9-11). Later, he issues the same command to Jairus's dead daughter: "Child, get up [*egeire*]!" The girl gets up (*anestē*) at once (Luke 8:54-55//Mark 5:41-42).

When Jesus sets his sights on Jerusalem, Luke begins to evoke the vocabulary and plot of 2 Kgs. 2:1-12. Jesus starts his journey as the days approach for him to be "taken up [*analēmpseōs*]" (Luke 9:51). As we have seen, Luke reinforces this vocabulary with two allusions to Elijah's ministry: a question about inhospitable Samaritans and another about family obligations for disciples (Luke 9:52-56, 61-62). Together with Jesus' forty days in the wilderness, his encounter with God on a mountain, and his reviving three children, these allusions establish Jesus as a prophet like Elijah with followers like Elisha.

Luke can now show how God transfers Jesus' spirit to the disciples just as God transferred Elijah's spirit to Elisha. To accomplish this, Luke first makes a

---

7. For the similar Elijah miracles, see 1 Kgs. 17:1-16; 2 Kgs. 2:8.

8. Cf. 1 Kgs. 17:17-24.

significant change to Mark's crucifixion scene. According to Mark, the dying Jesus quotes Ps. 22:1: "My God, my God, why have you forsaken me?" (Mark 15:34). According to Luke, however, he quotes Ps. 31:5: "Father, into your hands I commend my spirit [*pneuma*]" (Luke 23:46). Then, after his resurrection, Jesus commands his chosen apostles to wait in Jerusalem. Referring to a prophecy of John the Baptist, he tells them, "You will be baptized with the Holy Spirit [*en pneumati baptisthēsesthe hagiō*]" (Acts 1:5).[9] Jesus, who relinquished his spirit on the cross, has now set the stage for his apostles to receive that same spirit.

Allusions to 2 Kings 2 pepper the opening chapters of Acts.[10] They begin in the first sentence of Acts with a brief mention of "the day when [Jesus] was taken up [*analēmphthē*]" (Acts 1:2). Luke then recounts the scene: as the disciples converse with Jesus in Jerusalem, he is lifted up into a cloud. They are watching (*blepontōn*) and "gazing up toward heaven [*atenizontes . . . eis ton ouranon*]" as he vanishes from their sight (Acts 1:6-11). Two men inform the disciples, "This Jesus, who has been taken up from you into heaven [*analēmphtheis aph' hymōn eis ton ouranon*], will come in the same way as you saw [*etheasasthe*] him go into heaven [*eis ton ouranon*]" (Acts 1:11). Luke underscores the key phrase once more in Peter's final reference to "the day when he was taken up from us [*analēmphthē aph' hymōn*]" in Acts 1:22. Jesus has left his disciples in much the same manner as Elijah left Elisha. They must now wait for the promised Spirit.

The very next episode takes place on the day of Pentecost. Jesus' followers—men and women, as foretold in Joel 2:28-29—are gathered together in Jerusalem (Acts 1:14). A wind from heaven sweeps through their house. Illuminated by tongues of fire, they are "filled with the Holy Spirit [*eplēsthēsan . . . pneumatos hagiou*]" and begin to speak in other languages (Acts 2:2-4). This confuses their fellow Jews, many of them pilgrims celebrating the festival. Why are these Galileans speaking in the languages of Mesopotamia, Asia Minor, North Africa, Arabia, and Rome? Are they drunk? Peter clears up their confusion with his inaugural sermon (Acts 2:14-40). As with Jesus' inaugural sermon (Luke 4:16-30), the text is a prophecy about the Holy Spirit, a prophecy now being fulfilled: "In the last days it will be, God declares, that I will pour out my Spirit upon all flesh, and your sons and daughters shall prophesy. . . . Even upon my slaves, both men and women, in those days I will pour out my Spirit; and they shall prophesy" (Acts 2:17-18; cf. Joel 2:28-29).[11] The transfer is now

---

9. Cf. Luke 24:49. Luke borrows John the Baptist's saying from Mark (Mark 1:8//Luke 3:16).

10. Luke Timothy Johnson, *Luke-Acts: A Story of Prophet and People* (Chicago: Franciscan Herald, 1981), 42; Johnson, *The Acts of the Apostles*, SP 5 (Collegeville, MN: Liturgical, 1992), 30–31.

complete. Peter and the apostles are Spirit-filled prophets, ready—like Elisha—to carry on the ministry of their mentor.

Their ministry develops along similar lines. Like Jesus, they have received the Holy Spirit and preached a sermon about it. Now they concentrate on saving sinners.[12] Peter begins the process in his first sermon with this stern accusation: "Therefore let the entire house of Israel know with certainty that God has made him both Lord and Messiah, this Jesus whom you crucified" (Acts 2:36). "When they heard this," Luke reports, "they were cut to the heart."[13] "What should we do?" they ask (Acts 2:37). The very same question is put to John the Baptist at the beginning of Luke's Gospel (Luke 3:10). Accordingly, Peter gives a good John-the-Baptist answer: "Repent, and be baptized every one of you in the name of Jesus Christ so that your sins may be forgiven; and you will receive the gift of the Holy Spirit. For the promise is for you, for your children, and for all who are far away, everyone whom the Lord our God calls to him" (Acts 2:38-39). By inviting "every one," Peter casts a wide net. The haul: "about three thousand persons" (Acts 2:41).

Peter follows his Jesus-like sermon with Jesus-like miracles. The first involves a paralyzed beggar. "I have no silver or gold," he says, "but what I have I give you; in the name of Jesus Christ of Nazareth, stand up and walk [egeire kai peripatei]" (Acts 3:6).[14] Peter then raises (ēgeiren) the man, who begins to walk (peripatein), leap, and praise God (Acts 3:8-9).[15] Like Jesus, Peter heals a paralytic—clear evidence that Peter has received the spirit of Jesus just as Elisha received the spirit of Elijah.[16]

---

11. Lucien Cerfaux, "Témoins du Christ d'après le Livre des Actes," in Recueil Lucien Cerfaux, BETL 6–7 (Gembloux: J. Duculot, 1954), 2:164–66; Johnson, Luke-Acts, 26. Johnson and Beverly Roberts Gaventa note that Luke adds the phrase "they shall prophesy" to Acts 2:18 (see Johnson, Acts of the Apostles, 49; Gaventa, The Acts of the Apostles, ANTC [Nashville: Abingdon, 2003], 77).

12. See also Paul S. Minear, To Heal and to Reveal: The Prophetic Vocation According to Luke (New York: Seabury, 1976), 147.

13. When Elijah confronts Ahab over Naboth's vineyard, he elicits a similar reaction: Ahab is "cut to the heart [katenugē]" (1 Kgs. 21:27).

14. The words egeire kai are present in Codex Alexandrinus but missing from manuscripts like Codex Sinaiticus and Codex Vaticanus. They could easily have been added by scribes familiar with Matt. 9:5; Mark 2:9; Luke 5:23; and John 5:8. On the other hand, they could have been omitted because they seem to contradict the fact that the man does not get up on his own (Acts 3:7). Either way, the discrepancy does not affect my conclusion that Luke uses the verbs egeirein and peripatein to link Luke 5:23-24 with Acts 3:5-9. See Bruce M. Metzger, A Textual Commentary on the Greek New Testament (Stuttgart: United Bible Societies, 1971), 307.

15. The verb is used three times: peripatei/peripatōn/peripatounta. Codex Bezae omits the phrase "walking and leaping (peripatōn kai hallomenos kai)."

In the power of that spirit, Peter goes on to heal many others. Like Jesus, he restores another paralytic and raises a woman from the dead (Acts 9:32-43).[17] Like Jesus, he knows people's thoughts and pronounces judgments. For example, Ananias and Sapphira withhold some money intended for distribution among needy Christians. They cannot hide from Peter, however. He accuses them of conspiracy and sentences them to death: "How is it that you have agreed together to put the Spirit of the Lord to the test? Look, the feet of those who have buried your husband are at the door, and they will carry you out" (Acts 5:8-9). The grim prediction is immediately fulfilled.

Now that Luke has characterized Peter as a prophet like Jesus just as Elisha was a prophet like Elijah, he can use Peter as an agent for ministry to Gentiles. Just as God sent Elijah to a Sidonian widow and Elisha to a Syrian leper, God will now send Peter to a Roman centurion. Guided by the same Spirit, Philip will go to an Ethiopian eunuch and Paul will proclaim the good news to Gentiles from Antioch to Rome. Meanwhile, however, Jerusalem Jews will reject Peter and the other apostles. The prophet who sets that precedent is neither Elijah nor Elisha. It is Moses.

16. For similar arguments, see F. F. Bruce, *Commentary on the Book of Acts* (London: Marshall, Morgan & Scott, 1954), 85; Lampe, "The Holy Spirit in the Writings of Luke," 177; Charles H. Talbert, *Literary Patterns, Theological Themes and the Genre of Luke-Acts* (Missoula, MT: Scholars Press, 1974), 16; Johnson, *Acts of the Apostles*, 71.

17. See also Adrian Hastings, *A Prophet and Witness in Jerusalem: A Study of the Teaching of Saint Luke* (London: Longmans, Green, 1958), 74; Dubois, ""La Figure d'Elie," 174; Johnson, *Acts of the Apostles*, 180.

8

Rejected Prophets

In chapter 5, we saw how Luke depicts immediate and consistent Jewish rejection. Starting with Jesus' sermon in Nazareth and ending with his crucifixion in Jerusalem, Jews object to his sabbath breaking, his assumption of God's prerogative to forgive sins, and his gestures toward Gentile inclusion. They challenge him; they conspire against him; they arrest him; they mistreat him; they condemn him; they accuse him to Pilate; they demand his execution. This is a shocking outcome for God's Messiah. Luke, however, assures his audience that Jewish rejection is part of God's plan. Prophets like Simeon and Jesus foretell Jewish rejection all along. Moreover, the Scriptures anticipate the Messiah's rejection and vindication. David himself says that the people of Israel, along with the Gentiles and their rulers, set themselves against God's Messiah. They are the "builders" who reject God's "cornerstone."

In Luke's view, this is not so unusual. Jesus is a prophet, and Israel has always rejected God's prophets. Isaiah and Jeremiah explain why: they do not truly listen because they cannot understand. We noted in chapter 5 that this pattern applies particularly to the prophet like Moses foretold in Deut. 18:15, 18-19. For Luke, Jesus is the prophet like Moses—the prophet about whom God says, "You shall listen to him." The people, however, reject Moses after he strikes down an Israelite's Egyptian oppressor. Likewise, they reject Jesus after he strikes down unclean spirits, disease, sin, and death. In the words of Stephen, "He supposed that his kinsfolk would understand that God through him was rescuing them, but they did not understand" (Acts 7:25).

Because Peter is a prophet like Jesus, he will also face rejection by his own people. Luke takes great pains to demonstrate that this, too, is part of God's plan. Drawing on Mark and Q, he shows how Jesus prophesies Jewish rejection of Peter and the apostles. Three of Jesus' parables indicate that even after the Jerusalem establishment has condemned Jesus, they will have a second chance to accept the good news of God's salvation. This lays the foundation for Luke to complete his portrait of Jesus and his apostles as prophets like Moses. Just as the Israelites rejected Moses twice—first in Egypt, then in the wilderness—so the Jerusalem authorities will reject first Jesus, then Peter and the apostles.

"YOU SHALL LISTEN"

Luke's Jesus first prophesies the apostles' rejection in the Beatitudes, borrowed from Q (Luke 6:20-23//Matt. 5:1-12). Jesus tells them, "Blessed are you when people hate you, and when they exclude you, revile you, and defame you on account of the Son of Man. Rejoice in that day and leap for joy, for surely your reward is great in heaven; for that is what their ancestors did to the prophets" (Luke 6:22-23). This statement not only forecasts slander and ostracism for the apostles but also compares their rejection to the rejection of Israel's prophets. Next, Luke begins to echo rejection themes from Mark. Jesus sends out the twelve disciples with instructions for dealing with rejection: they must shake the dust of inhospitable towns from their feet (Luke 9:5//Mark 6:11). He prophesies his own rejection, then tells his disciples that they, too, must carry their cross. They must risk their lives to follow him (Luke 9:23-24//Mark 8:34-35).[1]

As Jesus begins his journey to Jerusalem, he appoints seventy disciples—a gesture that likens them to the seventy elders appointed by Moses (Luke 10:1; cf. Num. 11:16). After instructing them, he pronounces woes against the Galilean cities that will reject them (Luke 10:13-15//Matt. 11:20-24). These woes, copied from Q, are followed by this statement: "Whoever listens [akouōn] to you listens [akouei] to me, and whoever rejects you rejects me, and whoever rejects me rejects the one who sent me" (Luke 10:16). A similar statement appears in Matthew: "Whoever welcomes you welcomes me, and whoever welcomes me welcomes the one who sent me" (Matt. 10:40). If this statement comes from Q, then Luke has either retained or substituted vocabulary that best suits his purposes. The issue for Luke is not so much whether Israel welcomes the apostles but whether Israel listens to them or rejects them.

This issue seems to lie behind Luke's version of Q's woe to the descendants of the prophets' murderers. Three differences between Luke and Matthew's versions highlight Luke's concerns. First, Luke's Jesus levels an accusation not found in Matthew: "You are witnesses [martyres] and approve [syneudokeite] of the deeds of your ancestors [paterōn]; for they killed them, and you build their tombs" (Luke 11:48). Second, while Matthew designates God's emissaries as "prophets, sages, and scribes," Luke calls them "prophets and apostles" (Matt.

---

1. See also Robert C. Tannehill, *The Narrative Unity of Luke-Acts: A Literary Interpretation* (Philadelphia: Fortress Press, 1986), 1:287.

23:34; Luke 11:49). Third, Luke alone identifies their sender as "the Wisdom of God": "The Wisdom of God said, 'I will send [*apostelō*] them prophets [*prophētas*] and apostles [*apostolous*], some of whom they will kill and persecute'" (Luke 11:49). Whom does Luke quote here? Who is "the Wisdom of God"? As we have seen, Luke may be thinking of God's word according to Jeremiah and 2 Chronicles:

> From the day that your ancestors [*pateres*] left the land of Egypt until this day, I sent [*exapesteila*] to you all my servants the prophets [*prophētas*]. I sent [*apesteila*] them all day and at dawn the next day, yet they did not listen [*ēkousan*] to me. They did not turn their ears and they stiffened their necks more than their ancestors [*pateras*]. So you will speak to them this word: "This is the nation that did not listen [*ēkousen*] to the voice of the Lord." (Jer. 7:25-28)

> I kept sending [*apestellon*] to you my servants the prophets [*prophētas*]. Even though I sent them at dawn, you did not listen [*eisēkousate*] and you did not incline your ears when they said, ". . . Do not go after other gods to serve them and bow down to them, lest you make me angry by the work of your hands." (Jer. 25:4-6)

> He sent to them prophets [*apesteilen pros autous prophētas*] to turn them to the Lord but they did not listen [*ouk ēkousan*]. They warned them but they did not listen [*ouk ēkousan*]. (2 Chron. 24:19)

With its references to prophets and apostles, its evocation of prophecy about ancestors who did not listen, and its accusation against those who witness and approve of their deeds, Luke's version points forward not only to Jesus' rejection but also to the rejection of the apostles.[2] When God sends his apostles and prophets, many will do as their ancestors did. Instead of listening and understanding, they will persecute and kill. They will bear witness to the deeds of other persecutors and murderers—and they will approve of those deeds.

As we shall see, all this happens to God's prophets and apostles: to Peter, John, Stephen, James, and Paul. In Paul's case, it begins in Acts 7:58; 8:1 with his approving (*syneudokōn*) the murder of Stephen and guarding the coats of the witnesses (*martyres*). Luke also uses Mark to forecast the rejection of

---

2. See also Paul S. Minear, *To Heal and to Reveal: The Prophetic Vocation According to Luke* (New York: Seabury, 1976), 124.

God's prophets and apostles. He changes two verses from Mark in which Jesus warns his disciples of persecution. "When they bring you to trial" becomes "when they bring you before the synagogues, the rulers, and the authorities" (Mark 13:11//Luke 12:11-12); "they will hand you over to councils; and you will be beaten in synagogues; and you will stand before governors and kings" becomes "they will arrest you and persecute you; they will hand you over to synagogues and prisons, and you will be brought before kings and governors" (Mark 13:9//Luke 21:12). As Luke tells the story, it is synagogues and prisons, rulers and authorities, kings and governors that will arrest and persecute Jesus' witnesses.[3]

Why do they arrest and persecute? It is because they do not listen. Luke gets this idea from Israel's Scriptures. He highlights two passages in particular. Twice, he quotes from God's word to Moses in Deut. 18:15, 18-19:

> The Lord your God will raise up [*anestēsei*] a prophet like me from your people. You shall listen [*akousesthe*] to him. . . . I will raise up [*anastēsō*] for them a prophet like you from among their people; I will put my words in his mouth and he will speak to them as I command him. Any person who does not listen [*akousē*] whatever that the prophet speaks in my name, I will myself will punish that person. (cf. Acts 3:22; 7:37)

Isaiah 6:9-10 also receives two explicit citations:
> Go to this people and say,
> "You will indeed listen [*akoē akousete*] but never understand;
>   you will indeed look [*blepontes blepsete*] but never perceive.
> For this people's heart has grown dull,
>   and their ears are hard of hearing [*ēkousan*],
>   and they have shut their eyes,
>   so that they might not look [*idōsin*] with their eyes,
>   and listen [*akousōsin*] with their ears,
>   and understand with their heart and turn—
>   and I would heal them." (Acts 28:26-27; cf. Luke 8:10)

These two passages, enhanced by the allusions to Jeremiah and 2 Chronicles in Luke 11:49, explain everything for Luke. Jesus is the prophet like Moses, foretold in Deut. 18:15-20. God raises him up from among the Jewish people,

---

3. See also Jerome Neyrey, *The Passion According to Luke: A Redaction Study of Luke's Soteriology* (New York: Paulist, 1985), 84–88; Tannehill, Ibid., 1:246.

and the people must listen to him. Yet many of them cannot truly listen. They are stubborn, and their ears are hard of hearing. They will not turn and be healed.[4]

If Jesus is the prophet like Moses, Luke reasons, then God must give Israel two opportunities to listen: once with Jesus himself; again with Jesus' witnesses. Luke lays out the logic in Stephen's speech (Acts 7:23-43). Before Stephen takes the stage, however, Luke foreshadows the two opportunities in three of Jesus' parables. The first is the parable of the Barren Fig Tree (Luke 13:6-9). We have already noticed that when the tree misses its first opportunity to bear fruit, the owner gives it another chance.

The second parable, the parable of the Great Dinner, probably comes from Q (Luke 14:15-24//Matt. 22:1-10). As with the parable of the Talents/Pounds, the two versions share a similar story line. In this case, a host whose dinner guests refuse his invitation sends his servants to invite anyone they can find. The two versions differ significantly in detail, however. For our purposes, the relevant difference concerns the number of servants and the number of times the host sends them out. In Matthew's version, several servants go first to the invited guests and then to the thoroughfares. According to Luke, however, one servant makes three trips. The first two times, he stays inside the town, calling the invited guests and then bringing in "the poor, the crippled, the blind, and the lame" from the "avenues and alleyways." He then goes "out into the roads and the country lanes" (Luke 14:21-23, my translation). Before he extends his mission into the countryside, he gives the town-dwellers a second invitation. In the same way, before Peter and the apostles extend the offer of salvation to the Gentiles, they will give Jews a second chance.[5]

The final "second chance" parable, told to Pharisees, is found only in Luke. It contrasts the fate of a rich man with that of Lazarus, the poor man who used to beg at his gate. In the afterlife, Lazarus rests in Abraham's bosom while the rich man suffers in Hades. The rich man begs Abraham to send Lazarus to his brothers "that he may warn them, so that they will not also come into this place of torment." In essence, the rich man is asking for a second chance. Abraham's answer, however, is not very encouraging. "They have Moses and the prophets," he says. "They should listen [*akousatōsan*] to them." "No," says the rich man, "but if someone goes to them from the dead, they will repent." "If they do not listen [*akouousin*] to Moses and the prophets," replies Abraham,

4. David L. Tiede and Donald Juel also comment on the importance of Deut. 18:15-20 and Isa. 6:9-10 (see Tiede, *Prophecy and History in Luke-Acts* [Philadelphia: Fortress Press, 1980], 40-42; Juel, *Luke-Acts: The Promise of History* [Atlanta: John Knox, 1983], 109-11).

5. See also Luke Timothy Johnson, *The Gospel of Luke*, SP 3 (Collegeville, MN: Liturgical, 1991), 222.

"neither will they be convinced even if someone rises [*anastē*] from the dead" (Luke 16:27–31).

"Listen to What I Say"

When Jesus rises from the dead, the Pharisees—and indeed all Jews—have another opportunity to repent. Peter gives them that opportunity in his first two speeches (Acts 2:38–40; 3:19). Thousands jump at the chance. They repent and receive baptism for the forgiveness of their sins (Acts 2:41, 47; 4:4). The Jerusalem authorities, however, continue to resist. They arrest Peter three times. They interrogate him; they flog him; they plan to execute him. They reject Peter as they rejected Jesus and Moses before him.[6]

Peter becomes a prophet like Moses just as he becomes a prophet like Elijah: he receives the spirit of his teacher and prophesies (Acts 2:1–4; cf. Num. 11:16–17, 24–25). He gives Jerusalem its chance at repentance in his inaugural speech. This speech is perhaps most famous for its argument that the crucified Jesus is in fact the Messiah. The thesis comes toward the end: "Let the entire house of Israel know with certainty [*asphalōs*] that God has made him both Lord and Messiah, this Jesus whom you crucified" (Acts 2:36). It rounds off convincing scriptural proofs for "the certainty [*asphaleian*] concerning the things [Luke's audience has] been taught" (Luke 1:4).

The speech presents other proofs in allusions that portray Jesus and Peter as prophets like Moses. They start with Peter's quotation of Joel's prophecy about "portents [*terata*] in the heaven . . . and . . . on the earth," inserting the important phrase "and signs [*kai sēmeia*]" (Acts 2:19). He then describes Jesus as "a man attested to you by God with deeds of power, wonders, and signs [*terasi kai sēmeiois*] that God did through him among you" (Acts 2:22). This is the first of ten references that link Jesus and his apostles to Moses, famous for the "signs and wonders [*sēmeia kai terata*]" he performed in Egypt.[7] Here, it leads to an accusation: "This man, handed over to you according to the definite plan and foreknowledge of God, you crucified and killed" (Acts 2:23). Like Moses, Jesus is a rejected prophet. Moreover, as with Moses, "God raised him up [*anestēsen*]" (Acts 2:24). This is so important that Peter says it twice: "This Jesus God raised up [*anestēsen*]" (Acts 2:32). He then gives his audience an opportunity to "repent and be baptized . . . that your sins may be forgiven" (Acts 2:38). The Jews Peter has just accused of crucifying the Messiah are getting a second chance.

---

6. Tannehill, *Narrative Unity of Luke-Acts*, 2:68.

7. The other nine references to *terata kai sēmeia* are found in Acts 2:43; 4:30; 5:12; 6:8; 7:36; 8:6, 13; 14:3; 15:12.

Peter's second speech contains fewer explicit messianic proofs and more explicit Moses references. It follows an interval where the apostles, like Moses and Jesus, do "wonders and signs [*terata kai sēmeia*]" (Acts 2:43).[8] These include Peter's healing the paralytic (Acts 3:1-10). The astonishment of Jewish bystanders provides the occasion for the speech. Once more, Peter accuses his audience: they "rejected [Jesus] in the presence of Pilate"; they "rejected the Holy and Righteous One" whom God "raised [*ēgeiren*] from the dead" (Acts 3:13-15). This time, however, Peter explains why they did it. They and their rulers "acted in ignorance" (Acts 3:17). Peter therefore offers them a second chance. "Repent," he says, "and turn to God so that your sins may be wiped out, so that times of refreshing may come from the presence of the Lord, and that he may send the Messiah appointed for you" (Acts 3:19).

Those who accept Peter's offer will enter into the fullness of the messianic age. Those who refuse, however, will suffer the worst consequence imaginable. According to Luke, this consequence is spelled out in Moses' warning to Israel: "The Lord your God will raise [*anestēsei*] up for you from your own people a prophet like me. You must listen [*akousesthe*] to whatever he tells you. And it will be that everyone who does not listen [*akousē*] to that prophet will be utterly rooted out of the people" (Acts 3:22-23; cf. Deut. 18:15, 19). Jesus, of course, is the prophet whom God "raised up [*anestēsen*]." Having used this verb twice in his first speech, Peter will now add it to the final appeal of his second speech: "You are the descendants of the prophets and of the covenant that God gave to your ancestors, saying to Abraham, 'And in your descendants all the families of the earth shall be blessed.' When God raised up [*anastēsas*] his servant, he sent him first to you, to bless you by turning you from your wicked ways" (Acts 3:26). The choice is clear. Repentance will lead to forgiveness, times of refreshing, the sending of God's Messiah, and the blessing promised to Abraham in Gen. 22:18. If Jerusalem's Jews do not listen, however, they will suffer the curse pronounced on Abraham's uncircumcised descendants (Gen. 17:14) and Israelites who eat leaven during Passover (Exod. 12:15, 19). They "will be utterly rooted out of the people" (Acts 3:23).[9]

Peter gives his third and fourth speeches to the Jerusalem council. These speeches are occasioned by his first two arrests: one in response to the commotion caused by the second speech; the other in response to further

---

8. Tannehill, *Narrative Unity of Luke-Acts*, 2:32.

9. Luke Timothy Johnson, *The Literary Function of Possessions in Luke-Acts*, SBLDS 39 (Missoula, MT: Scholars Press, 1977), 65–66; Johnson, *The Acts of the Apostles*, SP 5 (Collegeville, MN: Liturgical, 1992), 80. Luke likely conflates Deut. 18:19 with Gen. 17:14; Exod. 12:15, 19 on the basis of similar sentence structure and the fact that both curses involve not listening to Moses.

"wonders and signs [*terata kai sēmeia*]" performed through the apostles (Acts 5:12). Both times, Peter stands before the council with its elders and chief priests who question him much as they questioned Jesus.[10] Jesus' prophecy in Luke 12:11-12 is being fulfilled—especially since (according to Acts 4:8) the Holy Spirit is teaching Peter what he ought to say. His defense speeches follow a familiar pattern: Peter accuses his audience of having crucified the Messiah; he states that God has "raised [*ēgeiren*]" Jesus (Acts 4:10; 5:30); he claims that through Jesus God forgives and saves Israel. Neither speech presents the council with an opportunity to repent. The council has quite another decision to make. "What will we do with them?" they ask (Acts 4:16).

In the end, the Pharisee Gamaliel provides the solution. Rising up (*anastas*) to address the council (Acts 5:34), Gamaliel warns that if the movement led by the apostles is "of God," the council should not—and indeed cannot—resist it (Acts 5:39). On the other hand, if it is "of human origin," it is destined to fail (Acts 5:38). Gamaliel supports his argument with two examples of similar movements that did fail. First Theudas, then Judas the Galilean "rose up [*anestē*]" and gained a following.[11] Eventually, however, each was killed and "all who were convinced by [*epeithonto*] him" were scattered (Acts 5:36-37, my translation). The council is "convinced [*epeisthēsan*]" by Gamaliel's argument (Acts 5:39). They do not hand the apostles over to the Romans. Instead, they inflict on them a punishment that Pilate had suggested for Jesus. They flog the apostles and then release them.[12]

What does Gamaliel really prove? He suggests that the Jesus movement, like the Theudas and Judas movements, will probably die out. Luke's audience, however, knows better. They believe that the Jesus movement is "of God." This is why it thrives in their day, years after Gamaliel and even the Jerusalem council have died out. With this in mind, Luke punctuates Gamaliel's speech with verbs that signal the unexpected outcome. Gamaliel uses the verbs *anistanai* and *peithein* to describe Theudas and Judas. Both "rose up" and "convinced" many followers. They perished and their followers disbanded. Luke subtly undermines Gamaliel's argument by using the same verbs to describe Gamaliel.

10. Compare Acts 4:5-7; 5:27-28 to Luke 22:66-68.

11. Gamaliel's speech is notoriously anachronistic. According to Josephus (*Ant.* 20.97–99), the procurator Fadus ordered an attack on the followers of a false prophet named Theudas, along with the execution of their leader, sometime between 44 and 46 CE. The setting of Acts 5, however, predates 44 CE (the death of Herod Agrippa in that year is not described until Acts 12:20-23). In addition, Gamaliel places the activity of Judas the Galilean after the death of Theudas. In fact, Judas' rebellion occurred in 6 CE.

12. Compare Luke 23:16, 22 with Acts 5:40.

Gamaliel, too, "rose up"—to address the Jerusalem council. Gamaliel, too, "convinced" his followers—the council members. In this way, Luke implicitly compares Gamaliel to Theudas and Judas. Gamaliel, too, will perish and the council will be disbanded. Their undertaking, it seems, is "of human origin."

This is not the case with the Jesus movement, says Luke. When Jesus is killed, his followers do not disperse. They do not scatter until Stephen is killed—but even then, the movement does not die out. Instead, it keeps growing (Acts 8:1, 12, 38; 9:18, 42; 10:48).[13] Now, about fifty years later, the Romans have executed Peter and Paul. Still, unlike those convinced by Theudas, Judas, and even Gamaliel, those convinced by Jesus, Peter, and Paul continue to multiply. Clearly, their undertaking is "of God." They can be killed and they can be scattered, but they cannot be overthrown.

Luke's wordplay takes on even more significance in light of his previous use of the verbs *anistanai* and *peithein*. The former is important because it describes the prophet like Moses—the prophet whom the Lord will "raise up [*anastēsei*]," identified as Jesus in Acts 3:22; 7:37. Altogether, Luke uses the verb ten times with reference to Jesus.[14] It therefore seems shortsighted of Gamaliel to use it with reference to Theudas and Judas. This impression is strengthened when we reconsider the parable of the Rich Man and Lazarus, a parable addressed to Pharisees that ends on this note: "If they do not listen to Moses and the prophets, neither will they be convinced [*peisthēsontai*] even if someone rises [*anastē*] from the dead" (Luke 16:31). The Pharisee Gamaliel and the Jerusalem council are like the rich man's brothers. They are not convinced even by the prophet like Moses who rises from the dead.

"THEY COVERED THEIR EARS"

Stephen brings the conflict to a head. He enters the story because of a dispute among the Jewish believers in Jerusalem. Hellenistic (Greek-speaking) widows are receiving less food than Hebrew (Aramaic-speaking) widows (Acts 6:1-6). The apostles, reluctant to "neglect the word of God," appoint seven men (Hellenistic Jews, judging by their names) "to wait [*diakonein*] on tables" (Acts 6:2). The scene is reminiscent of Moses' appointing seventy elders in response

---

13. See also Johnson, *Acts of the Apostles*, 102–3; John A. Darr, "Irenic or Ironic? Another Look at Gamaliel before the Sanhedrin (Acts 5:33-42)," in *Literary Studies in Luke-Acts*, ed. Richard P. Thompson and Thomas E. Phillips (Macon, GA: Mercer University Press, 1998), 121–39; Jack Dean Kingsbury, "The Pharisees in Luke-Acts," in *The Four Gospels 1992*, ed. Frans van Segbroeck et al., BETL 100 (Leuven: Leuven University Press, 1992), 2:1503–7.

14. Luke 9:22; 18:33; 24:7, 46; Acts 2:24, 32; 3:26; 13:33–34; 17:3, 31.

to the people's complaints about the food ration (Num. 11:10-30). When the elders assume responsibility, the Lord takes some of the spirit that is on Moses and puts it on them (Num. 11:17, 25). Later, Moses gives some of his authority to Joshua—"a man in whom is the spirit"; a man "full of the spirit of wisdom"—by laying hands on him (Num. 27:18-23; Deut 34:9).[15]

Accordingly, Stephen—one of the seven *diakonoi*, "full of the Holy Spirit and of wisdom"—becomes a prophet like Moses through the laying on of the apostles' hands (Acts 6:5-6). Like Moses, Jesus, and Peter before him, he does "wonders and signs [*terata kai sēmeia*]" (Acts 6:8). As Jesus promised in Luke 12:11-12, "the Spirit" enables him to confound his opponents (Acts 6:10). Still, Stephen's arguments get him into trouble. Other Hellenistic Jews arrange to have him brought up before the council on a capital charge: blasphemy against Moses and God. In response, he makes a lengthy speech.

Stephen does not so much defend himself against blasphemy as turn the charge against the council.[16] His discourse leads to this indictment: "You stiff-necked people, uncircumcised in heart and ears, you are forever opposing the Holy Spirit, just as your ancestors used to do. Which of the prophets did your ancestors not persecute? They killed those who foretold the coming of the Righteous One, and now you have become his betrayers and murders. You are the ones that received the law as ordained by angels, and yet you have not kept it" (Acts 7:51-53). The indictment levels two accusations: they have murdered God's Messiah, and they have not kept the law. The first resonates strongly with Jesus' prophecy against the lawyers: "You build the tombs of the prophets whom your ancestors killed. So you are witnesses and approve of the deeds of your ancestors; for they killed them, and you build their tombs. Therefore also the Wisdom of God said, 'I will send them prophets and apostles, some of whom they will kill and persecute'" (Luke 11:47-49). Jesus' woe and Stephen's speech establish Jewish rejection of God's Messiah as part of a pattern—a pattern that will extend to Jewish rejection of the apostles. The pattern can be expressed in a simple syllogism: Jesus and his witnesses are prophets; Israel persecutes and kills the prophets; therefore, the Jerusalem council will persecute and kill Jesus and his witnesses.

The speech begins with a long discourse that lays a foundation for both accusations. Since Stephen wants to argue that history is repeating itself, he makes two claims: first, that Israel's ancestors always rejected prophets in the same way that the council has now rejected Jesus; second, that in doing so they

---

15. Johnson, *Acts of the Apostles*, 107.

16. Neyrey agrees with this assessment, going so far as to claim that the trial of Stephen becomes the trial of Israel (*The Passion According to Luke*, 94).

broke God's law. He therefore summarizes Israel's history with these ends in view.[17] He begins by recalling God's promises to Abraham (Acts 7:2-8). God told Abraham that his descendants would inherit "the land in which [Jews] are now living" (Acts 7:4; cf. Gen. 13:15; 17:8; 48:4). Then, no matter what, God kept faith with Abraham. Even when Abraham had no descendants, God gave him Isaac, Jacob, and the twelve patriarchs (Acts 7:5, 8). Even when they became slaves in Egypt, God rescued them and made another promise: "They shall come out and worship me in this place" (Acts 7:7).[18]

What, then, happened with Abraham's descendants? Did they keep faith with God and worship him in Jerusalem?[19] Not at all, says Stephen. The very first Israelites rejected their very first prophet when the patriarchs sold their brother Joseph (Acts 7:9-16). God, however, did not abandon Joseph or his brothers. Because God rescued Joseph from his afflictions and Pharaoh appointed him ruler over Egypt, Joseph was able to save his starving brothers—the very ones who sold him—by inviting them to share his grain reserves in Egypt. Although Israel's initial rejection of Joseph got them off to a bad start, the episode ended well. The patriarchs accepted Joseph's invitation to live in Egypt. They did not reject him a second time.

Their descendants, however, were less receptive to Moses, the prophet who dominates the remainder of Stephen's discourse (Acts 7:17-50). Having set the stage with God's promise of rescue from Egypt and worship in Jerusalem followed by Israel's rejection of their very first prophet, Stephen now summarizes Exodus 1–32, using specific details to make three points. First, he shows how God acted to fulfill the twofold promise to Abraham, appointing Moses for two tasks: to save Israel from oppression and to command them concerning worship. Second, he emphasizes how the people rejected Moses both times. Third, he demonstrates how their descendants continue to reject Moses. Along the way, Stephen draws implicit comparisons between Moses and Jesus, further substantiating his point that the council's rejection of Jesus follows a well-established pattern.

---

17. Juel, *Luke-Acts*, 71–72. Juel compares Stephen's speech to other biblical speeches that rehearse history in order to make a point (e.g., Josh. 24:2-15; Neh. 9:6-37; Ps. 78; Dan. 9:4-19).

18. The quotation conflates Gen. 15:13-14; Exod. 3:12; and Deut. 12:5-6. In Deut. 12:5, Moses implicitly identifies the "place" as Jerusalem. Luke introduces God's promise to Abraham of rescue and worship (Gen. 15:13-14) in Zechariah's prophecy (Luke 1:73-75). Here, Stephen accuses the council of breaking God's commandment as articulated in Exod. 3:12 and Deut. 12:5-6. See Nils Alstrup Dahl, "The Story of Abraham in Luke-Acts," in *Jesus in the Memory of the Early Church* (Minneapolis: Augsburg Press, 1976), 74; Tannehill, *Narrative Unity of Luke-Acts*, 2:92–93.

19. Juel also identifies the fulfillment of God's promise as Stephen's central concern (*Luke-Acts*, 72).

Stephen begins the Moses story with a reminder that God was about to fulfill the promise concerning worship in Jerusalem (Acts 7:17). He then introduces God's agent Moses. Moses was "instructed in all . . . wisdom," "powerful in his words and deeds" (Acts 7:22). In a first bid to rescue Israel, he defended a Hebrew slave. "He supposed that his kinsfolk would understand that God was bringing them salvation through him, but they did not understand" (Acts 7:25, my translation). "Who made you a ruler [*archonta*] and a judge over us?" one of them asked as he "pushed Moses aside" (Acts 7:27).[20]

In response to this first rejection, Moses left the scene. After forty years, however, God appeared to Moses "in the flame of a burning [*pyros*] bush" (Acts 7:30). This time, God sent Moses "as both ruler [*archonta*] and redeemer [*lytrōtēn*]" (Acts 7:35, my translation). Moses led the people out of Egypt, performing "wonders and signs [*terata kai sēmeia*]" (Acts 7:36). On Mount Sinai, he received God's word—presumably including the commandment not to make an idol—and relayed it to the people. Nevertheless, they "rejected" him a second time (Acts 7:35). They were "unwilling to obey him"; "they pushed him aside" (Acts 7:39). Instead, they "made a calf [*emoschopoiēsan*], offered sacrifice [*anēgagon thusian*] to the idol, and reveled in the works of their hands [*tois ergois tōn cheirōn autōn*]" (Acts 7:41).[21]

Stephen explains that the golden calf episode was not a temporary lapse from which the people quickly recovered. It was the beginning of a trend. "God turned away from them and handed them over to worship the host of heaven" so that their idolatry continued for the next forty years "in the wilderness [*en tē erēmō*]."[22] Although they had the "tent [*skēnēn*] of testimony" that God told Moses to "make [*poiēsai*] . . . according to the pattern [*typon*] he had seen," they did not offer "sacrifices [*thysias*]" to God. Instead, according to Amos 5:25-27, they "took along the tent [*skēvēv*] of Moloch . . . and the images [*typous*] that [they] made [*epoiēsate*] to worship" (Acts 7:42-43).

These people have a terrible record. They rejected God's prophets: Joseph, once; Moses, twice. Instead of obeying the commandment, they made a calf. Instead of sacrificing at the tent of testimony, they sacrificed at the tent of

20. Stephen quotes Exod. 2:14.

21. Here Stephen's vocabulary echoes the story of the golden calf: "He took [the gold rings] from their hands [*ek tōn cheirōn autōn*] . . . and made [*epoiēsan*] them into the cast image of a calf [*moschon*]. . . . They brought [*prosēnegken*] a sacrifice [*thysian*]" (Exod. 32:4, 6). It also evokes one of Jeremiah's oracles: "And I will speak to them with judgment because they forsook me and sacrificed [*ethysan*] to other gods and bowed down to the works of their hands [*tois ergois tōn cheirōn*]" (Jer. 1:16).

22. The phrase "host of heaven" (*stratia tou ouranou*) is borrowed from Jer. 7:18; 8:2; 19:13.

Moloch. They made images and reveled in the works of their hands. Why should anyone think that they would change their ways when Moses' tent gives way to Solomon's temple (Acts 7:45-47)? Will that house, "made with human hands [cheiropoiētos]," be the fulfillment of God's promise of "worship . . . in this place [topō]" (Acts 7:7, 48)? No, says Stephen, this time citing Isa. 66:1-2. Human hands cannot presume to build a "place [topos]" of rest for God whose "hand [cheir]" has "made [epoiēsen]" heaven and earth (Acts 7:49-50).[23] Just because Jerusalem has made a temple and adorned it with beautiful stones and gifts dedicated to God does not mean that God will dwell there—especially if it is no longer a house of prayer but rather a den of robbers. The temple authorities may think they are worshiping God, but in reality they are continuing the trend that started with the golden calf. They are worshiping the works of their hands.[24]

Stephen has proved his second accusation: like their ancestors, the council has not kept the law. As for the first accusation—that they murdered the Messiah—Stephen has been proving it all along with subtle comparisons: Joseph and Moses on the one hand; Jesus and the apostles on the other. Like Joseph, Jesus was rejected by his fellow Israelites only to be rescued by God (Acts 7:9; cf. 2:22-24; 3:13-15; 4:10; 5:30; 13:27-30).[25] Just as Pharaoh appointed Joseph ruler over Egypt, so God exalted Jesus and made him "both Lord and Messiah" (Acts 7:10; cf. 2:33, 36; 5:31).[26] Just as Joseph offered salvation to the very ones who sold him, Jesus' apostles have offered salvation to the very ones who killed him (Acts 7:14; cf. 2:38-40; 3:19-20).[27]

The comparisons extend to Moses, who—as Stephen reminds the council—said, "God will raise up a prophet for you from your own people as he raised me up" (Acts 7:37; cf. Deut. 18:15). Like Moses, Jesus is "instructed in all . . . wisdom" and "powerful in his words and deeds" (Acts 7:22; cf. Luke 2:40, 52; 24:19).[28] Like Moses, Jesus performs "signs and wonders [terata kai sēmeia]" (Acts 7:36; cf. 2:22).[29] Like Moses, Jesus "supposed that his kinsfolk would understand [synienai] that God was giving them salvation [sōtērian] through

23. In Acts 17:24, Paul makes a similar remark about Athenian shrines.

24. Juel, Luke-Acts, 75.

25. See also F. F. Bruce, Commentary on the Book of Acts (London: Marshall, Morgan & Scott, 1954), 151; Richard I. Pervo, Acts: A Commentary, Hermeneia (Minneapolis: Fortress Press, 2008), 181–82.

26. For a similar interpretation, see Beverly Roberts Gaventa, The Acts of the Apostles, ANTC (Nashville: Abingdon, 2003), 124.

27. See also Bruce, Commentary on the Book of Acts; Johnson, Acts of the Apostles, 121–22.

28. See also Pervo, Acts, 184.

29. See also Johnson, Acts of the Apostles, 50; Pervo, Acts, 187.

him, but they did not understand [*synēkan*]" (Acts 7:25, my translation). Indeed, Jerusalem Jews "acted in ignorance" when they killed Jesus, the "savior [*sōtēr*]" and "redemption [*lytrōsin*] of Jerusalem" (Luke 2:11, 38; Acts 3:17; 4:12).[30]

This is just what Isaiah prophesied in a verse so important to Luke that he quotes it twice: "You will indeed listen but never understand [*synēte*]" (Isa. 6:9). The first quotation refers to Jewish rejection of Jesus (Luke 8:10). The second quotation (Acts 28:26-27) refers to Jewish rejection of the apostles. According to Stephen, this second rejection resembles the second rejection of Moses.[31] Just as God waited forty years to send Moses "as both ruler [*archonta*] and redeemer [*lytrōtēn*]," so God waited forty days to exalt Jesus "as Leader [*archēgon*] and Savior [*sōtēra*]" (Acts 7:35; cf. 1:3; 5:31). Just as God sent the message of rescue by Moses from "the flame of a burning [*pyros*] bush," so God has sent the message of "repentance to Israel and forgiveness of sins" by apostles baptized "with the Holy Spirit and fire [*pyri*]" (Acts 7:30, 35, cf. Luke 3:16; Acts 2:3-4, 5:31). Both Moses and the apostles perform "wonders and signs [*terata kai sēmeia*]" (Acts 7:36; cf. 2:43; 4:30; 5:12). The Jerusalem council, however, has rejected the apostles. They are "stiff-necked . . . uncircumcised in heart and ears" (Acts 7:51).[32] They have always persecuted God's prophets, including Joseph and Moses. Accordingly, they have persecuted and killed God's Messiah, the prophet Jesus.[33]

What is more, they will now persecute and kill Stephen. From their perspective, Stephen is guilty of the charges against him. He has spoken against Moses and the temple. From Luke's perspective, however, Stephen is a prophet. He is a prophet like Zechariah, killed by "stoning [*elithoboloun*]" in Jerusalem (Acts 7:57, 59).[34] He is also a prophet like Jesus, "full . . . of the Holy Spirit," doing "great wonders and signs [*terata kai sēmeia*]" and inciting his opponents to a murderous rage (Acts 6:5, 8; 7:54-55; cf. Luke 4:14, 28-29; Acts 2:22). His trial before the Jerusalem council resembles the trial that Luke knows from Mark's story. The charge is blasphemy; the evidence comes from false witnesses; the defendant speaks of Christ at God's right hand; he is then convicted and

---

30. See also Tannehill, *Narrative Unity of Luke-Acts*, 2:91. Luke frequently uses cognates of *sōzein* and *lytrousthai* to describe Jesus and his mission. See Luke 1:68-69, 71, 77; 2:11, 38; 24:21; Acts 4:12; 5:31; 13:23, 26. In Acts 13:27, Luke repeats the idea that Jerusalem Jews killed Jesus out of ignorance.

31. See also Bruce, *Commentary on the Book of Acts*, 153; Johnson, *Literary Function of Possessions*, 75; Johnson, *Acts of the Apostles*, 136.

32. Here Stephen borrows vocabulary from Deut. 10:16; Isa. 63:10, and Jer. 6:10 (LXX).

33. Juel, *Luke-Acts*, 73–74, 110; Neyrey, *The Passion According to Luke*, 94, 96.

34. There is one major difference: while Zechariah prays for vengeance, Stephen calls down forgiveness. Compare 2 Chron. 24:22 with Acts 7:60.

executed (Acts 6:11-14; 7:54-58; cf. Mark 14:55-64). When he dies, he surrenders his spirit (Acts 7:59; cf. Luke 23:46).[35]

By stoning Stephen, the council members prove themselves guilty as charged. They have persecuted and killed God's prophets. They reject Jesus as their ancestors rejected Joseph. They reject Jesus and his witnesses as their ancestors twice rejected Moses.[36] They "[cover] their ears [*syneschon ta ōta autōn*]" (Acts 7:57) as did their ancestors in the time of Kings Joash and Jehoiakim. When Joash ruled, God "sent prophets to them [*apesteilen pros outous prophētas*], to turn them to the Lord, but they did not listen [*ouk ēkousan*]. [The prophets] testified against them, but they did not listen [*ouk ēkousan*]. . . . They set upon [Zechariah] and . . . stoned [*elithobolēsan*] him in the court of the house of the Lord" (2 Chron. 24:19, 22). When Jehoiakim was king, God said through Jeremiah, "I kept sending [*apestellon*] to you my servants the prophets [*prophētas*]. Even though I sent them at dawn, you did not listen [*eisēkousate*] and you did not incline your ears [*proseschete tois ōsin hēmōn*] when they said, '. . . Do not go after other gods to serve them and bow down to them, lest you make me angry by the work of your hands [*tois ergois tōn cheirōn*]'" (Jer. 25:4-6). Through Jesus, God now explains that they are liable for more than murdering Jesus and Stephen: "The Wisdom of God said, 'I will send them prophets and apostles [*apostelō eis autous prophētas kai apostolous*], some of whom they will kill and persecute,' so that this generation may be charged with the blood of all the prophets shed since the foundation of the world, from the blood of Abel to the blood of Zechariah, who perished between the altar and the sanctuary. Yes, I tell you, it will be charged against this generation" (Luke 11:49-51). From Luke's perspective, the sentence has already been carried out. The Romans have destroyed the temple, doing away with the functional priesthood and the Jerusalem council. As Gamaliel had so unwittingly predicted, their movement has died out.

---

35. Henry J. Cadbury, *The Making of Luke-Acts*, 3rd ed. (Peabody, MA: Hendrickson, 1999), 231; Tannehill, *Narrative Unity of Luke-Acts*, 2:99; Johnson, *Acts of the Apostles*, 112–13; Gaventa, *Acts of the Apostles*, 131–32. Stephen's cry, "Lord, do not hold this sin against them," probably does not run parallel to Jesus' prayer, "Father, forgive them; for they do not know what they are doing" (Acts 7:60; Luke 23:34). The prayer from Luke does not seem to have been original to the Gospel, as several "early and diverse witnesses" do not include it (Bruce M. Metzger, *A Textual Commentary on the Greek New Testament* [Stuttgart: United Bible Societies, 1971], 180).

36. Johnson, *Literary Function of Possessions*, 76; Johnson, *Acts of the Apostles*, 137; Tannehill, *Narrative Unity of Luke-Acts*, 2:68.

9

"To the Ends of the Earth"

Stephen's death sets up a new procedure for Jesus' witnesses. Having been rejected by Jews, they turn to non-Jews. Jesus foreshadows this modus operandi in his inaugural sermon. "No prophet is accepted in the prophet's hometown," he says, and goes on to describe how the prophets Elijah and Elisha were sent not to Israelites but to Gentiles (Luke 4:24-27). As we have seen, however, Jesus himself has no contact with Gentiles. Neither do his followers, until after Stephen is killed. Then, to escape persecution, "all except the apostles" leave Jerusalem (Acts 8:1). The good news is beginning to spread into Judea and Samaria. Soon, it will reach the ends of the earth.

Luke makes it clear that Gentile inclusion has been part of God's plan all along. God's prophets, ancient and contemporary, have always said so. Luke quotes four passages in particular, two of them before Stephen dies. According to Isaiah, "All flesh shall see the salvation of God" (Luke 3:6; cf. Isa. 40:5). According to Joel, God will pour out the Holy Spirit "upon all flesh." This includes everybody: "both men and women," "everyone who calls upon the name of the Lord" (Acts 2:17-21; cf. Joel 2:28-32).

Interestingly, neither of these prophecies specifies Gentiles. When Peter cites Joel 2:28-32, only Jews are saved (Acts 2:41).[1] When Gentiles start to believe, however, Paul and James (the brother of Jesus) turn to two additional prophecies for an explanation. Paul applies Isa. 49:6 to himself and Barnabas:

> I have set you to be a light for the Gentiles,
>   so that you may bring salvation to the ends of the earth. (Acts
> 13:47)

Still, not all Jewish believers think that Gentiles need only to repent and be baptized. They call on James to require circumcision (Acts 15:1-35). James

---

1. See also Donald Juel, *Luke-Acts: The Promise of History* (Atlanta: John Knox, 1983), 63.

disappoints them, however. His decision not to "trouble those Gentiles who are turning to God" is based on Amos 9:11-12:

> After this I will return,
> and I will rebuild the dwelling of David, which has fallen;
>> from its ruins I will rebuild it,
>> and I will set it up,
> so that all other peoples may seek the Lord—
>> even the Gentiles over whom my name has been called.
>>> Thus says the Lord, who has been making these things known from long ago. (Acts 15:16-18)

Of course Gentiles will seek the Lord when the Davidic Messiah comes. God has been saying this all along.

Luke reinforces the message of ancient prophets with the forecasts of contemporary prophets. Simeon introduces the notion of Gentile inclusion by recognizing the infant Jesus as "a light of revelation to the Gentiles" (Luke 2:32). In this brief statement, he anticipates the work of Philip, Peter, and Paul. At the same time, he invokes Isa. 49:6: "I have set you to be a light for the Gentiles."[2]

Jesus also prophesies Gentile salvation. What he has hinted in his inaugural sermon he states more explicitly after his resurrection: the disciples will proclaim "repentance and forgiveness of sins . . . to all nations" (Luke 24:47). As foretold in Isa. 49:6, they will go "to the ends of the earth" (Acts 1:8). After his ascension, Jesus appears in a vision to Ananias, a believer in Damascus. He tells Ananias that Paul has been "chosen to bring [Jesus'] name before the Gentiles and kings and before the people of Israel" (Acts 9:15). This statement confers additional legitimacy on Paul's mission. Jesus himself associates Gentile inclusion specifically with Paul.

According to Jesus, Simeon, and the prophets, then, God's plan of salvation includes everyone, Jews and Gentiles alike. Now it is up to Jesus' witnesses to implement God's plan. Philip is the first to proclaim the good news to non-Jews. Next, Peter steps in to bestow apostolic approval on Samaritan and Gentile conversions.[3] This clears the way for Paul to bring the gospel to Asia Minor, Cyprus, Macedonia, Achaia, Crete, and Rome.

---

2. Acts 26:17-18, 23 also underscores the importance of Isa. 49:6.

3. Juel, *Luke-Acts*, 68–69, 105.

"The City of Samaria"

After Stephen's death, Philip leaves Jerusalem to proclaim the good news: first in "the city of Samaria"; then on the Jerusalem-Gaza road (Acts 8:1-40). Luke introduces Philip as another of the seven *diakonoi*—a prophet whom the apostles appoint just as Moses appointed the seventy elders (Acts 6:1-6). Luke further confirms Philip's likeness to Moses, Jesus, Peter, and Stephen by mentioning his "signs [*sēmeia*]" and great "deeds of power [*dynameis*]" (Acts 8:6, 13; my translation).[4] Philip proclaims the good news; he casts out unclean spirits; he heals paralytics; he draws large crowds. His prophetic powers assure Luke's audience that his baptizing Samaritan believers, "both men and women" (Acts 8:12), is part of God's plan. God moves to confirm this: they receive the Holy Spirit when the apostles send Peter and John to lay hands on them.[5] Peter and John then return to Jerusalem, preaching in Samaritan villages as they go.

Philip breaks evangelistic ground not only with Samaritans but also with a Gentile—the first Gentile in Luke-Acts to hear the good news. The details of Acts 8:26-40 assure the evangelist's audience that this, too, is part of God's plan. For one thing, the Lord orchestrates Philip's movements from beginning to end. "The angel of the Lord" directs him to the Gaza road; the Spirit leads him to the Ethiopian eunuch's chariot and whisks him away after the baptism.[6] For another thing, Luke portrays Philip as a prophet. Like Elijah, Philip gets up and goes in response to God's command (Acts 8:26-27; cf. 1 Kgs. 17:9-10). As with Elijah, the Spirit snatches Philip away (Acts 8:39; cf. 1 Kgs. 18:12).[7] Philip is also a prophet like Jesus. In fact, the entire episode runs parallel to Jesus' postresurrection encounter with Cleopas and the other disciple (Luke 24:13-35). In that story, Jesus meets the two disciples on the road to Emmaus. They have a question about Jesus' death, which Jesus answers by interpreting the Scriptures. The disciples invite Jesus to stay with them. Jesus then breaks bread and disappears, leaving two disciples with their hearts on fire. Similarly, Philip meets the Ethiopian eunuch on the Gaza road. The man invites Philip to sit in his chariot. He has a question about the Scriptures, which Philip answers

---

4. See also Robert C. Tannehill, *The Narrative Unity of Luke-Acts: A Literary Interpretation* (Philadelphia: Fortress Press, 1990), 2:104. Luke seems to associate *dynameis* with Jesus based on Mark 5:30 and Matt. 11:21//Luke 10:13. Jesus is full of *dynamis*: Luke 4:14, 36; 5:17; 6:19; Acts 10:38. His witnesses follow suit: Luke 24:49; Acts 1:8; 4:33; 6:8. According to Luke 19:37, Jesus performs *dynameis*. According to Acts 2:22; 19:11, so do the apostles and Paul.

5. See also Tannehill, *Narrative Unity of Luke-Acts*, 2:105.

6. See also ibid., 2:108.

7. Luke Timothy Johnson, *The Acts of the Apostles*, SP 5 (Collegeville, MN: Liturgical, 1992), 158.

by telling him about Jesus' death. Philip then baptizes the man and disappears, leaving one rejoicing eunuch.[8]

The turning point of the story is the eunuch's rhetorical question: "What is to prevent me from being baptized?" (Acts 8:36). Luke's audience can probably think of at least two things. For one, the man is an uncircumcised Gentile. For another, he is a eunuch, prohibited from converting to Judaism.[9] Yet here is an eager, God-fearing man instructed by a prophet like Moses and Jesus, a prophet led by the Spirit and the angel of the Lord. Here is some water. Luke's audience may well reply, "What indeed?"

"Even on the Gentiles"

Should they still have doubts, however, Luke will now lay them to rest. The next Gentile conversion will be the work of Peter (Acts 10:1-48). As in the story of Philip and the Ethiopian eunuch, a Spirit-led prophet baptizes a God-fearing Gentile whose social position might cause Jewish Christians some concern. Unlike Philip, however, Peter is firmly established as an authoritative prophet and the leader of the Jerusalem apostles. Peter has inherited Jesus' Spirit and performed Jesus' miracles. In case Luke's audience has forgotten all this, Luke reminds them in the scenes leading to the encounter with Cornelius.[10] First, Peter heals yet another paralyzed man (Acts 9:32-35). He then raises a dead woman. The scene is reminiscent of the Elijah and Elisha resuscitation stories: the corpse lies "room upstairs [hyperōon]"; the prophet enters the room alone; he prays; the dead person's eyes open (Acts 9:37-40; cf. 1 Kgs. 17:19; 2 Kgs. 4:10, 32-35).[11] It also resembles the stories of Jairus's daughter and the widow's son at Nain: loved ones make a desperate entreaty; mourners weep; the prophet tells the corpse to get up; with the prophet's assistance, the dead person complies (Acts 9:38-41; cf. Luke 7:14; 8:41, 52-55).[12] Peter continues to perform the

---

8. F. Scott Spencer, *The Portrait of Philip in Acts*, JSNTS 67 (Sheffield: JSOT Press, 1992), 141–44.

9. Lev. 21:20; Deut. 23:1; Josephus, *Ant.* 4.290–91.

10. See also Beverly Roberts Gaventa, *The Acts of the Apostles*, ANTC (Nashville: Abingdon, 2003), 156.

11. See also Jean-Daniel Dubois, "La Figure d'Elie dans la Perspective Lucanienne," *RHPR* 53 (1973): 174; Richard I. Pervo, *Acts: A Commentary*, Hermeneia (Minneapolis: Fortress Press, 2008), 256n51.

12. It is interesting to note how Luke retains more of Mark's details for the Tabitha story than for his version of the Jairus story. In addition to the desperate entreaty, the weeping mourners, the command to get up, and the sitting up with assistance, Luke also notes that Peter "put all of them outside [ekbalōn de exō pantas]" and told the dead woman, "Tabitha, get up" (Acts 9:40; cf. Mark 5:40-41; see also Pervo, *Acts*, 254). Even when he is not trying to persuade his audience (who may or may not be familiar with Mark), Luke portrays Peter as a prophet like Jesus.

miracles of Elijah, Elisha, and Jesus. There can be no doubt that Peter carries on Jesus' prophetic ministry.[13]

Luke nevertheless shows that Peter's encounter with the Roman centurion Cornelius is entirely managed by God. First, an angel instructs Cornelius to send for Peter. Next, a voice commands Peter to eat unclean food: "What God has made clean, you must not call profane" (Acts 10:15).[14] Peter takes the lesson to heart. In obedience to the Spirit's direction, he enters Cornelius's home and proclaims the good news to everyone gathered there. Suddenly, the Holy Spirit falls on these new believers. Peter then asks the critical question: "Can anyone withhold the water for baptizing these people who have received the Holy Spirit just as we have?" (Acts 10:47).

How will Luke's audience respond this time? At stake is not just one controversial convert on his way to Ethiopia but a contingent of the Roman occupying force in Caesarea. Still, they are God-fearing people. God clearly orchestrates the whole scene. God's emissary is Jesus' most prominent successor, a visionary prophet guided by the Holy Spirit. Moreover, even if Luke's audience balks at accepting Cornelius and his household, the Jerusalem apostles will not. The command to eat unclean food; the lesson about defilement; the Spirit's direction; the angel sent to Cornelius; the gift of the Holy Spirit—all this is enough to persuade them that "God has given even to the Gentiles the repentance that leads to life" (Acts 11:18).[15]

At the Jerusalem council, Peter will use this evidence to persuade them again (Acts 15:6-11). Meanwhile, he must play out a final rejected prophet scene (Acts 12:1-19). The conflict begins when Herod Agrippa I executes James the son of Zebedee. This pleases the Jews, so Herod arrests Peter. Peter's third arrest looks like it may be his last. Herod intends to execute Peter as he executed James.

What Herod does not know is that Peter is a prophet like Jesus. Arrested during the Festival of Unleavened Bread and waiting to be brought before the people, Peter will escape from prison and foil the Roman ruler's plot (see Luke 22:7, 54; 23:13; 24:1-12).[16] It becomes a kind of resurrection scene. Night has fallen and Peter is sleeping in his cell. An angel appears and says, "Get up [anasta]" (Acts 12:7; cf. Luke 24:7). The first witness to Peter's escape is a

---

13. See also Tannehill, *Narrative Unity of Luke-Acts*, 2:126–27; Johnson, *Acts of the Apostles*, 178–80.

14. Luke seems to have transferred this lesson from Mark 7:15: "There is nothing outside a person that by going in can defile." For Mark, it paves the way for Jesus to meet a Syrophoenician woman. For Luke, it prepares Peter to meet a Roman centurion.

15. See also Tannehill, *Narrative Unity of Luke-Acts*, 2:133; Juel, *Luke-Acts*, 105–6.

16. See also Tannehill, *Narrative Unity of Luke-Acts*, 2:153.

woman. When she tells the believers that Peter is at the gate, nobody believes her. Peter then appears to them, saying, "Tell this to James and to the believers" (Acts 12:17; cf. Luke 24: 5-11). Peter's rising from his cell looks remarkably like Jesus' rising from his tomb.[17]

The scene takes on even more poignancy when we try reading it through the eyes of Luke's audience, living in the 80s. Peter had been dead some twenty years, most likely executed in Rome under Nero after the great fire of 64. An audience with this in mind might see Peter's arrest and imminent execution in the early 40s as a preview of events in the mid-60s. What would they make of his miraculous escape? Perhaps they would recognize it as a metaphor for his ultimate destiny: raised from the dead, Peter leaves them and goes to another place (Acts 12:17). For Luke's audience, the entire episode seems to mix a tender tribute to a beloved hero with the assurance that God always vindicates God's prophets.[18]

"THEY WILL LISTEN"

It also assures Luke's audience that, even after a crisis involving Peter, "the word of God continued to advance and gain adherents" (Acts 12:24). Now that Philip and Peter have baptized an Ethiopian eunuch and the household of Cornelius, Paul will proclaim the gospel all over the Gentile world. Unlike Philip and Peter, however, Paul does not belong to the community of believers in Jerusalem. He does not have their apostolic credentials. Luke therefore stresses that God works through Paul just as God works through Peter and Philip.[19] Paul, too, receives instructions from the Holy Spirit and voices that come to him in visions (Acts 9:3-6; 13:2; 16:6-7, 9; 18:9-10; 19:21; 22:17-21; 23:11; 27:23-24). Paul, too, is a prophet. After opposing Jesus, he receives a prophetic commission. Filled with the Holy Spirit, he preaches an inaugural sermon, heals a paralytic, and raises a dead man. Just as Elijah transferred his spirit to Elisha, Jesus has transferred the Holy Spirit to Peter—and now to Paul.[20]

Paul seems an unlikely candidate. Luke introduces him at the stoning of Stephen, where Paul (Saul) guards the coats of the "witnesses [*martyres*]" (Acts 7:58). He "approved [*syneudokōn*] of their killing him," says Luke (Acts 8:1). His betrayal of Stephen is even worse than Peter's betrayal of Jesus. Peter

17. See also Johnson, *Acts of the Apostles*, 218; Pervo, *Acts*, 308–9.

18. See also Pervo, *Acts*, 309–10.

19. Luke Timothy Johnson, *Luke-Acts: A Story of Prophet and People* (Chicago: Franciscan Herald, 1981), 48–51; Juel, *Luke-Acts*, 79–81.

20. Johnson, *Acts of the Apostles*, 226.

simply denies any association with the condemned man (Luke 22:54-62). Paul, however, colludes with the witnesses and approves the murder. As if that were not enough, Paul goes on to persecute other believers, dragging them off to prison and threatening them with execution (Acts 8:3; 9:1-2). This makes him subject to Jesus' accusation: "You are witnesses [*martyres*] and approve [*syneudokeite*] of the deeds of your ancestors; for they killed [the prophets]" (Luke 11:48). Paul is now liable for "the blood of all the prophets" (Luke 11:50).

What turns him around is a prophetic call (Acts 9:3-9).[21] It follows a familiar pattern: the prophet experiences a theophany; God commissions the prophet; God enables the prophet. Paul's theophany consists of a blinding light and the voice of the risen Jesus. Luke includes details that stress the typical nature of this theophany: the divine voice twice pronounces the prophet's name; the encounter leaves the prophet prostrate (Acts 9:4).[22] It also echoes familiar themes. Although Paul can "see [*eblepen*] nothing" and remains three days "without sight [*mē blepōn*]," he has "heard [the] voice [*ēkousen phōnēn*]" of the "Lord [*kyrie*]" (Acts 9:4-9; cf. Isa. 6:9-10; Jer. 7:25-28).[23] Jesus tells Paul to wait for further instructions. It is then up to Ananias to convey the commission and facilitate the enabling.

Ananias's involvement boosts Paul's credibility. The Damascus disciple raises the issue on everyone's mind: Paul has done "much evil" to believers in Jerusalem and now has authority "to bind all who invoke [Jesus'] name" in Damascus (Acts 9:14). Why lay hands on such a man? The risen Jesus responds with Paul's commission: "He is an instrument whom I have chosen to bring my name before Gentiles and kings and before the people of Israel; I myself will show him how much he must suffer for the sake of my name" (Acts 9:15-16).[24] This commission indicates that Paul's prophetic career will round off two of Luke's main themes: Gentile inclusion and Jewish rejection.[25] God enables Paul for this career by sending Ananias to baptize him. Once "something like scales"

21. See also Paul S. Minear, *To Heal and to Reveal: The Prophetic Vocation According to Luke* (New York: Seabury, 1976), 142.

22. Gerhard Lofink, *The Conversion of St. Paul: Narrative and History in Acts*, trans. and ed. Bruce J. Malina (Chicago: Franciscan Herald, 1976), 71; Gaventa, *Acts of the Apostles*, 148-49. Paul retells the story in Acts 22:1-16; 26:12-23.

23. See also Pervo, *Acts*, 685. It is worth observing that both Mark and Luke use blind and deaf characters to illustrate Isa. 6:9-10. Mark features two blind men and one deaf man whom Jesus heals (Mark 7:31-37; 8:22-26; 10:46-52). Luke retains only the second blind man story, inserting it after a comment about the disciples' misunderstanding (Luke 18:34-43). He then adds the story of Saul.

24. Luke repeats this prophecy in Acts 13:46-47; 20:22-23; 22:15-21; 26:16-17.

25. See also Tannehill, *Narrative Unity of Luke-Acts*, 2:119-20.

falls away from Paul's eyes, he sees and (one presumes) understands. He is filled with the Holy Spirit—the Spirit relinquished by Jesus at his death and now poured out on Peter, Stephen, Philip, and the other apostles.[26] Paul especially resembles Peter, the betrayer of a martyr who later takes over the martyr's ministry. Luke makes it difficult to doubt that Paul is an authentic prophet.

It is even more difficult to doubt when Paul, introduced as a prophet in Acts 13:1, preaches his inaugural sermon in Acts 13:13-41. Paul's inaugural sermon is much like those of Jesus and Peter (Luke 4:16-30; Acts 2:14-40).[27] Like Jesus, Paul gives the sermon in a synagogue. This synagogue, however, is nowhere near Nazareth. It is in Pisidian Antioch, a Roman colony in southeastern Asia Minor, where the Sabbath congregation includes Hellenistic Jews as well as Gentile converts to Judaism. Like Peter, Paul tells these Jews the story of Jesus: God sent him as the prophesied Messiah; Jerusalem Jews did not recognize him; they condemned him to death; God raised him from the dead; the apostles now offer Israel a second chance to receive forgiveness by believing in Jesus. For Paul, the offer comes with a warning. His audience should avoid the fate of the Israelites addressed in Hab. 1:5:

> Look, you scoffers!
> Be amazed and perish,
> for in your days I am doing a work,
> a work that you will never believe, even if someone tells you.
> (Acts 13:40)[28]

Will the Jews of Pisidian Antioch reject Paul just as the Jews of Jerusalem rejected Jesus and the apostles? Will they refuse to believe, even though Paul is telling them all about God's work? The episode ends for Paul much as similar episodes ended for Jesus and Peter. At first, the people hear him eagerly. Yet when Paul begins to draw a crowd, the unbelieving Jews "reject" him as their ancestors rejected Moses (Acts 13:46; cf. 7:27).[29] Paul then turns to the Gentiles. He proclaims the good news to both men and women (Acts 16:11-40; 17:12, 34). Unbelieving Jews, however, continue to make trouble for him. They

---

26. Charles H. Talbert, *Literary Patterns, Theological Themes and the Genre of Luke-Acts* (Missoula, MT: Scholars Press, 1974), 23; Johnson, *Acts of the Apostles*, 237.

27. Adrian Hastings, *A Prophet and Witness in Jerusalem: A Study of the Teaching of Saint Luke* (London: Longmans, Green, 1958), 136; Talbert, *Literary Patterns*, 23; Johnson, *Acts of the Apostles*, 237.

28. See also Juel, *Luke-Acts*, 81, 110–11.

29. See also Tannehill, *Narrative Unity of Luke-Acts*, 2:96, 168; Luke Timothy Johnson, *The Gospel of Luke*, SP 3 (Collegeville, MN: Liturgical, 1991), 237.

persecute him; they run him out of their towns; they stone him (Acts 13:50; 14:5, 19). Paul will be kicked out of synagogues from Iconium to Lystra; from Thessalonica to Beroea; in Corinth and Ephesus (Acts 14:1-2, 19; 17:5, 13-14; 18:6-7; 19:9). Once again, God's people reject God's prophet—and every time, he turns to Gentiles (Acts 18:6; 19:8-10; 22:21-22; 26:20-23; 28:23-28).

As Paul goes on to evangelize Gentiles, Luke consistently portrays him as a prophet like Jesus and Peter. He exhibits supernatural knowledge and imprecatory power when, filled with the Holy Spirit, he pronounces a judgment oracle on the false prophet Elymas (Acts 13:6-12; cf. Luke 4:1-13; Acts 5:1-11; 8:18-24). He performs "signs and wonders [sēmeia kai terata]" (Acts 14:3; 15:12). One of them—the healing of a paralytic—proves once and for all that he has inherited the spirit of Jesus and Peter (Acts 14:8-10; cf. Luke 5:17-26; Acts 3:1-10).[30] Luke signals the connection with characteristic details: the man's lifelong paralysis; Paul's intent gaze; the command to "stand upright"; the jumping up (halasthai) and walking (peripatein); the ensuing confusion among the bystanders as to the power at work. Eventually, Paul will complete the regimen of Jesus and Elijah miracles by raising a man who fell to his death from an "upper room [hyperōō]" (Acts 20:8-12).[31]

Like Jesus and Peter, Paul is eventually arrested by the Jerusalem authorities.[32] By now, Luke's audience expects nothing less. Jesus has prophesied persecution, arrest, and trial before "the synagogues, the rulers, and the authorities" as well as "kings and governors" (Luke 12:11-12//Mark 13:9).[33] He has told Ananias, "I myself will show [Paul] how much he must suffer for the sake of my name" (Acts 9:16).[34] So far, the prophecies have been fulfilled. Paul has been persecuted and arrested. He has been tried before magistrates, city authorities, and the proconsul of Achaia (Acts 13:50; 14:5, 19; 16:20-24; 17:5-9, 13; 18:12; 19:9, 23-27). Surely he will court trouble in Jerusalem. Because he is a prophet, Paul realizes this. In his farewell speech to the Ephesian elders, he states, "I am on my way to Jerusalem, not knowing what will happen to me there, except that the Holy Spirit testifies in every city that imprisonment

---

30. See also Henry J. Cadbury, *The Making of Luke-Acts*, 3rd ed. (Peabody, MA: Hendrickson, 1999), 232; Tannehill, *Narrative Unity of Luke-Acts*, 2:50–52, 177–78; Johnson, *Acts of the Apostles*, 251; Gaventa, *Acts of the Apostles*, 206–7.

31. See also Cadbury, *Making of Luke-Acts*, 232; Dubois, "La Figure d'Elie," 174; Talbert, *Literary Patterns*, 24; Tannehill, *Narrative Unity of Luke-Acts*, 2:127, 247–49; Johnson, *Acts of the Apostles*, 358; Gaventa, *Acts of the Apostles*, 279.

32. Hastings, *Prophet and Witness*, 136.

33. Ibid., 138.

34. See also Tannehill, *Narrative Unity of Luke-Acts*, 2:182.

and persecutions are waiting for me" (Acts 20:22-23). Agabus confirms this premonition with a prophetic action: he wraps Paul's belt around his feet and hands, saying, "This is the way the Jews in Jerusalem will bind the man who owns this belt and will hand him over to the Gentiles" (Acts 21:10-11).

The Jews in Jerusalem hand Paul over to the Gentiles because Paul is a prophet like Jesus. The parallels are hard to miss. They begin with Paul's conscious decision to travel to Jerusalem (Acts 19:21; cf. Luke 9:51).[35] They continue when he sends messengers ahead of him and foretells his sufferings (Acts 19:22; 20:22-23; cf. Luke 9:52; 18:31-33).[36] Paul's experience in "the city that kills the prophets" is remarkably like that of Jesus. Soon after his arrival, Paul is arrested (Acts 21:30; cf. Luke 22:54). Although the initial charges are brought by Hellenistic Jews, he winds up in Roman custody (Acts 21:27-36; cf. Luke 22:66—23:5). He appears before the Jerusalem council, two Roman governors, and King Herod Agrippa II (Acts 22:30—23:10; 24:1-23; 25:1-12; 25:23—26:32; cf. Luke 22:66—23:25).[37] Paul's defense before King Agrippa continues to affirm his prophetic identity. As Paul relates his prophetic call, he echoes the call narratives of Ezekiel and Jeremiah. "Stand on your feet [*stēthi epi tous podas*]," says the Lord (Acts 26:16; cf. Ezek. 2:1). "I am sending you [*egō apostellō se*]" to your people and to the Gentiles." "I will deliver you [*exairoumenos se*]" from them (Acts 26:17; cf. Jer. 1:7-8).[38]

From the standpoint of history, God does not deliver Paul. Just as Paul's journey to Jerusalem, arrest, and trials resemble those of Jesus, so does his eventual fate.[39] In all likelihood, Paul was executed by the Romans sometime after the fire of 64. Luke, however, finishes the story with events that took place early in the year 60. He brings Paul to Rome, but he does not narrate Paul's death. Instead, he ends as he began: with Jewish rejection, Gentile inclusion, and a quotation of Isa. 6:9-10. Paul—under house arrest, guarded by a soldier—spends his days with the Jews of Rome, arguing from the Scriptures that Jesus is the Messiah. Some are persuaded; others are not. This elicits his final statement, an affirmation of God's word as spoken through the prophet Isaiah:

---

35. Cadbury, *Making of Luke-Acts*, 232; Talbert, *Literary Patterns*, 16–17; Tannehill, *Narrative Unity of Luke-Acts*, 2:239; Johnson, *Acts of the Apostles*, 357.

36. Johnson, *Acts of the Apostles*, 358.

37. Cadbury, *Making of Luke-Acts*, 231; Hastings, *Prophet and Witness*, 138; Talbert, *Literary Patterns*, 17; Tannehill, *Narrative Unity of Luke-Acts*, 2:274, 345–46; Pervo, *Acts*, 533–34.

38. Robert F. O'Toole, *Acts 26: The Christological Climax of Paul's Defense (Ac. 22:11—26:32)*, AnBib 78 (Rome: Biblical Institute, 1978), 67.

39. Tannehill, *Narrative Unity of Luke-Acts*, 2:355.

Go to this people and say,
You will indeed listen [*akouē akousete*], but never understand,
    and you will indeed look, but never perceive.
For this people's heart has grown dull,
    and their ears are hard of hearing,
        and they have shut their eyes;
        so that they might not look with their eyes,
    and listen [*akousōsin*] with their ears,
and understand with their heart and turn—
    and I would heal them. (Acts 28:26-27)

This quotation rounds off a chorus of appeals to Israel. "You shall listen [*akousesthe*]," says Moses (Deut. 18:15). "Let anyone with ears to hear listen [*akouein akouetō*]!" calls Jesus (Luke 8:8). "Listen [*akouete*] to him!" says the voice from heaven (Luke 9:35). "Men of Judea and all who live in Jerusalem," says Peter, "listen [*enōtisasthe*] to what I say" (Acts 2:14). "You Israelites, and others who fear God," says Paul, "listen [*akousate*]" (Acts 13:16). God has faithfully raised up prophets and sent them to his people. Sadly, however, most of them do not listen.

Yet despite Jewish rejection and persecution to the death, Paul continues to proclaim the good news. "Let it be known to you then that this salvation of God has been sent to the Gentiles," he says. "They will listen [*akousontai*]" (Acts 28:28). The curtain closes on Paul proclaiming salvation to "all [*pantas*] . . . with all boldness and without hindrance" (Acts 28:30-31; cf. Luke 2:31). Luke's audience can be certain that God has set his apostles "to be a light for the Gentiles, so that [they] may bring salvation to the ends of the earth" (Acts 13:47; cf. Isa. 49:6). God sends them just as God has sent all the prophets. They are guided by angels; they are filled with the Holy Spirit; they fulfill the Scriptures; they fulfill Jesus' prophecies; they are prophets like Moses, Elijah, Elisha, Jeremiah, Ezekiel, and Jesus. They welcome all who come to them; they proclaim the kingdom of God; they seek out people who will listen.

Conclusion

If Jesus was the one to redeem Israel, why did the chief priests hand him over to be condemned and crucified? Why did Jesus eat and drink with tax collectors and sinners? Should uncircumcision prevent Spirit-filled Gentiles from being baptized? Why does the temple, adorned with beautiful stones and gifts dedicated to God, now lie in ruins with not one stone left upon another?

Luke-Acts endeavors to answer questions like these. Because each of them strikes at the heart of first-century Christian experience, Luke puts the answers in the mouths of prophets. "Thus it is written, that the Messiah is to suffer and rise from the dead on the third day" (Luke 24:46). "The Son of Man came to seek out and to save the lost" (Luke 19:10). "If then God gave them the same gift that he gave us when we believed in the Lord Jesus Christ, who was I that I could hinder God?" (Acts 11:17). "They will not leave within you one stone upon another; because you did not recognize the time of your visitation from God" (Luke 19:44). Even though it does not much look like the messianic age, Jesus is indeed the Messiah. Everything is proceeding according to God's plan.

These first-century questions and answers raise two important issues for twenty-first-century study of Luke-Acts. For one, they are not easily explained by the scholarly consensus that Luke, a Gentile, wrote to assure Gentiles of their salvation. According to Robert Maddox, "They are in danger of being persuaded that the division of Judaism and Christianity as distinct institutions might imply that Christians are excluded from the community of salvation."[1] "God's promises, after all, had been made to the people Israel," adds Luke Timothy Johnson. "If that historical people was not *now* in possession of the promised blessings, and someone else was, what did that signify for God's reliability?"[2]

Luke's questions and their answers do indeed offer an explanation for a hypothetical Gentile audience wondering about the certainty of their salvation. They portray Jewish rejection and Gentile inclusion as part of God's plan. Taken as a whole, however, they more plausibly reflect the concerns of first-century Jewish Christians. They are based on fundamental discrepancies between Jewish expectations and Christian teaching. They are Jewish questions

1. Robert Maddox, *The Purpose of Luke-Acts* (Edinburgh: T & T Clark, 1982), 183–84.

2. Luke Timothy Johnson, *The Writings of the New Testament: An Interpretation* (Philadelphia: Fortress Press, 1986), 203 (emphasis his).

posed by Jewish characters.[3] What is more, Luke supports his answers with testimony from authorities that would appeal to Jews: angels, the Holy Spirit, the Scriptures, first-century prophets, a voice from heaven. Could not Luke have been a Jew, writing for an audience of primarily Jewish Christians? Jacob Jervell, David Tiede, and Donald Juel have suggested as much.[4] Lukan scholarship would do well to reopen their line of inquiry.

A second issue raised by Luke's questions concerns their contemporary relevance. Thanks to Luke, Christians are no longer asking whether Jesus is the Messiah who forgives sins or whether uncircumcised Gentiles should be baptized. This does not mean, however, that questions about Jesus and salvation are irrelevant. They still address central issues for twenty-first-century Christians. When we wonder about Jesus' identity and mission, Luke's answers assure us of the certainty of what we have been taught. That God's Son seeks out and saves the lost; that he welcomes those who are estranged from God; that anyone can repent and be baptized—these tenets continue to elicit Christian faith and structure Christian catechesis.

Less relevant are questions about Jewish rejection and the destruction of the temple. When Luke addressed these questions, Jews who believed in Jesus were a distinct minority. They were vastly outnumbered and politically outgunned by Jews who did not believe. The deaths of prominent apostles and the Roman siege of Jerusalem were fresh in their minds. It made sense for them to understand Jewish rejection of Jesus, Peter, and Paul as the culmination of a long history of Jews rejecting their prophets. It made sense that this would have led to the destruction of the temple. After all, Israel's rejection of prophets like Moses and Jeremiah had led to the same result.

Today's circumstances are much different. Numerical and political advantage lies with Christians, most of whom are not Jewish. The Jewish War is long past. There is no urgent need to explain the destruction of the temple. Moreover, in the seventeen centuries since Constantine, Luke's answers have justified the oppression and mass slaughter of Jews who have had the misfortune to live among Christians. Only since World War II have some denominations eliminated liturgical language that emphasizes Jewish condemnation of Jesus,

3. In contrast, Gentile characters ask questions like, "What is to prevent me from being baptized?" (Acts 8:36). "What must I do to be saved?" (Acts 16:30). These questions are directed at Jews and cannot be properly answered until Jews are assured that "God has given even to the Gentiles the repentance that leads to life" (Acts 11:18).

4. Jacob Jervell, *Luke and the People of God: A New Look at Luke-Acts* (Minneapolis: Augsburg Press, 1972), 173–77; David L. Tiede, *Prophecy and History in Luke-Acts* (Philadelphia: Fortress Press, 1980), 1–10, 122; Donald Juel, *Luke-Acts: The Promise of History* (Atlanta: John Knox, 1983), 116–17.

often linking it to God's condemnation of the temple.[5] Auschwitz stands as a grim testimony to the evils fostered in a predominantly Christian society by Luke's answers concerning Jewish rejection of Jesus.

This is not to say, however, that Luke's answers are irrelevant in our day. The third evangelist still has something to say about the danger of rejecting God's prophet. We need only to hear it as a message to Christians rather than to Jews. Luke even invites us to do so. Although the warnings in his gospel pertain to Jews in particular, they can be easily construed as warnings for any dominant religious establishment. Consider the following examples: "It is written, 'My house shall be a house of prayer; but you have made it a den of robbers'" (Luke 19:46). "I will send them prophets and apostles, some of whom they will kill and persecute" (Luke 11:49). "Unless you repent, you will all perish just as they did" (Luke 13:3, 5). "Cut it down! Why should it be wasting the soil?" (Luke 13:7). Perhaps Luke is telling this story for the church.

He is certainly telling it for the church in the book of Acts. Ananias, Sapphira, and Simon the magician fall into the trap of loving money more than God—and they are believers (Acts 5:1-11; 8:9-24). According to Luke, the tendency is not limited to Pharisees. Christians, too, are inclined to admire their edifices, adorned with beautiful stones and gifts dedicated to God. Christians are inclined to revel in the works of their hands while neglecting justice and the love of God.

Luke's prophets have a word for such Christians. "Bear fruits worthy of repentance," says John the Baptist. (Luke 3:8). "Whoever has two coats must share with anyone who has none; and whoever has food must do likewise" (Luke 3:11). Jesus agrees: "When you give a banquet, invite the poor, the crippled, the lame, and the blind" (Luke 14:13). "Let the little children come to me, and do not stop them" (Luke 18:16). "Sell all that you own and distribute the money to the poor" (Luke 18:22). Peter and Paul take these lessons to heart. Peter refuses Simon's generous offer: "May your silver perish with you, because you thought you could obtain God's gift with money!" (Acts 8:20). Paul assures the Ephesian elders, "I coveted no one's silver or gold or clothing. You know

---

5. One popular hymn laments the doom of the sinners who rejected Jesus. In the 1940 hymnal of the Episcopal Church, their fate is described in this line: "Till not a stone was left on stone, and all a nation's pride, o'erthrown, went down to dust beside thee" (Walter Russell Bowie, Hymn 522 in *The Hymnal 1940* [New York: The Church Hymnal Corporation, 1961]). In the 1982 version, however, the bloodguilt is not limited to the nation whose temple was destroyed. The phrase "a nation's pride" has become "those nations' pride" (Bowie, alt., Hymn 598 in *The Hymnal 1982* [New York: The Church Hymnal Corporation, 1985]).

for yourselves that I worked with my own hands to support myself and my companions" (Acts 20:33-34).

Luke's prophets recall the church to Jesus' mission—a mission to bring good news to the poor; to heal the blind, the lame, the lepers, and the deaf; to raise the dead; to seek out and to save the lost; to proclaim repentance and forgiveness of sins in his name to all nations. Clothed with power from on high, Jesus' emissaries need no money or extra tunics. They need no barns full of grain and goods, no purple clothing or fine linen or sumptuous feasts. They have Moses and the prophets, including the prophet whom God raised from the dead. Let the church listen to them.

Index of Names

Index of Biblical References